TEACHING MATTERS

Also by Beverly Falk and Megan Blumenreich

The Power of Questions:
A Guide to Teacher and Student Research

TEACHING MATTERS

STORIES FROM INSIDE
CITY SCHOOLS

BEVERLY FALK AND MEGAN BLUMENREICH

with

Adesina Abani	*Neurys Bonilla*
Carol Castillo	*Evelyn Chang*
Joleen Hanlon	*Kanene Holder*
Laurie Jagoda	*Joan O'Brien*
Kisha Pressley	*lisa schaffner*
Rory Scott	*Travis Sloane*
Beatrice Tinio	*Hazel Veras-Gomez*

Mary Williams

20 YEARS

THE NEW PRESS

KH

Requests for permission to reproduce selections from this book should be
mailed to: Permissions Department, The New Press, 38 Greene Street,
New York, NY 10013.

Figs. 1–2 by Beatrice Tinio, used courtesy of the photographer
Figs. 3–11 by Travis Sloane, used courtesy of the photographer
Fig. 12 by Hazel Veras-Gomez, used courtesy of the photographer
Fig. 13 by Beverly Falk and Megan Blumenreich, used courtesy of the authors

Published in the United States by The New Press, New York, 2012
Distributed by Perseus Distribution

LIBRARY OF CONGRESS CATALOGING-IN-PUBLICATION DATA

Falk, Beverly.
Teaching matters : stories from inside city schools / Beverly Falk and
Megan Blumenreich with Adesina Abani ... [et al.].
p. cm.
Includes bibliographical references.
ISBN 978-1-59558-490-8 (pb : alk. paper)
1. Education, Urban--United States--Case studies. 2. Teachers--United
States--Case studies. 3. Children of minorities--Education--United
States--Case studies. I. Blumenreich, Megan. II. Abani, Adesina. III.
Title.
LC5141.F35 2012
370.9173'2--dc23
2012004564

Now in its twentieth year, The New Press publishes books that promote
and enrich public discussion and understanding of the issues vital to our
democracy and to a more equitable world. These books are made possible by
the enthusiasm of our readers; the support of a committed group of donors,
large and small; the collaboration of our many partners in the independent
media and the not-for-profit sector; booksellers, who often hand-sell
New Press books; librarians; and above all by our authors.

www.thenewpress.com

Book design and composition by Bookbright
This book was set in Janson Text

Printed in the United States of America

2 4 6 8 10 9 7 5 3 1

11/12/13

We dedicate this book to all the caring and committed teachers whose daily efforts are responsible for supporting children's learning and growth.

CONTENTS

It is rare that we get literally "inside" teaching to see not only *what* the problems of teaching are but *how* teachers learn to develop their own skills and abilities as they examine their own classrooms. And it is even rarer to see this kind of teaching and learning in urban classrooms. Falk and Blumenreich as well as their students teach us what it takes to inquire into one's own teaching and how this inquiry can be the source of deep and lasting learning.

In *Teaching Matters*, teachers struggle with the dilemmas of high-need urban communities. Rather than being stymied by them, however, they learn how to improve the learning of their students by enhancing their own teaching repertoires. Many of their students are immigrant children who come from different countries and cultures and who speak different languages. Teachers learn to create projects for them that integrate the disciplines—using poetry, art, and literature—as well as create community-oriented work that make students feel valued and appreciated for their differences.

To develop closer home/school partnerships, teachers study the parents as well as the children in their classes to find out what they care about, how they think, and what is important to them. As they get beneath the surface of people's lives, the teachers invent ways for parents to participate and for children to engage more fully by including ways for their cultural differences to become a part of classroom life.

These urban teachers pursue the questions that confront them: How do I teach my multiage dual-language classroom? How do I support literacy development in classrooms with English language learners? How do I create a curriculum that engages students when it is all scripted and tested? How can I bridge the competing demands of a test culture and the way children learn?

These teachers' inquiries teach us (and them) how to use the richness of their students' backgrounds, how to build stronger relationships with parents and families, how to enrich and differentiate instruction, as well as how to struggle with negotiating the constraints of mandates, scripts, and testing.

Read on and immerse yourself in an engrossing and deeply intelligent and emotional experience of how teachers examine their own practices. Learn from their inquiries how to *solve* the problems they are facing with strategies that help them confront rather than give up, that use differences as an asset rather than a problem, and that create, rather than negate, partnerships with parents as a way to connect them and their students to their schools.

Falk and Blumenreich join a growing movement of researchers who are finding out how to study and codify *teacher knowledge* as a way of gaining and documenting what teachers learn as they develop as educators—in this case, by providing them with the tools to examine and write about their own practices. This book is an outstanding contribution to that genre of research and one that you will reluctantly put down when you reach the last page.

—Ann Lieberman, Senior Scholar, Stanford University

ACKNOWLEDGMENTS

We are grateful to the teachers who participated in this project for agreeing to go public with their work. It has been our honor to collaborate with them and learn from them how to use inquiry to continually improve teaching. Thank you to Adesina Abani, Neurys Bonilla, Carol Castillo, Evelyn Chang, Joleen Hanlon, Kanene Holder, Laurie Jagoda, Joan O'Brien, Kisha Pressley, lisa schaffner, Rory Scott, Travis Sloane, Beatrice Tinio, Hazel Veras-Gomez, and Mary Williams.

How fortunate we are to teach and learn within the rich diversity of The City College of New York. Our students and colleagues provide a nourishing backdrop for our scholarship and daily work.

We extend special thanks to Ann Lieberman, our mentor and friend, whose life's work has been devoted to making teacher knowledge visible. Our research and teaching have been enriched not only by her pioneering efforts but also by her unfailing personal support.

Thank you as well to everyone at The New Press, especially our editor Marc Favreau and production editor Sarah Fan, for providing us with a home for this book and for supporting us through all the stages of publication. In addition, we wish to thank the book's copy editor, Cathy Dexter.

And to our families—Alan, Meryl, Luba, Thabiti, Anaiya, and Asa; Jon, Hank, and Maggie—we offer our deepest gratitude for all the encouragement, understanding, tolerance, and love that they so generously gift us with each day.

Questioning, Searching, Learning from Teaching

[T]here is no such thing as teaching without research and research without teaching. One inhabits the body of the other. As I teach, I continue to search and re-search. I teach because I search, because I question, and because I submit myself to questioning. I research because I notice things, take cognizance of them. And in so doing, I intervene. And intervening, I educate and educate myself. I do research so as to know what I do not yet know and to communicate and proclaim what I discover.

—Paulo Freire[1]

Teaching is a process of research. A good teacher listens to and observes her students, using this information to guide her instruction. This process of inquiring, collecting data, reflecting, and taking subsequent action is how teachers learn about what students know to support their optimal learning.

This book is based on the premise that an effective educator is continually engaged in the study of teaching and that inquiry about practice is an essential strategy for tackling the problems of schools and schooling, especially the complex problems found in the challenging contexts of diverse urban communities. Our perspective is grounded in what we consider to be essential purposes of education: to help learners acquire the knowledge, skills, and dispositions they will need to realize their potentials, find satisfaction and purpose in their lives, and participate fully in our democracy. Teaching to support these goals, we believe, involves providing opportunities for young learners to experience the power of posing questions about real-world problems and applying what they know to solve them—in much the same way we want them to do as active citizens in their adult lives.

In the pages that follow, we present stories of teachers who help students reach these goals by using the same skills that they seek to instill in their students to inquire about and grapple with dilemmas of their own teaching. The teachers featured in these stories come from diverse backgrounds— many that mirror those of their students—and thus have "insider" knowledge about them and the contexts in which they live. Their perspective on urban schooling is often quite different from that of "outside" educational researchers, or "experts"—those who most frequently inform the public about issues related to education. Typically, the average person learns about education through reports on how schools meet accountability measures that have been developed by policy makers with little experience or understanding of the teaching and learning process, especially of teaching and learning in the challenging contexts of high-need urban schools and communities. In such reports, it is currently popular to blame low student performance on teachers, unions, families, and students; favored responses for solving the problems are charter schools, business models for revamping school systems, and/or heroic individuals who "magically" motivate students to achieve. Little mention is made of the impact of poverty on students' learning (the fact that the United States has the highest child poverty rate—over 20 percent—of any industrialized nation in the world)[2] and little attention is given to the resources needed to close this "opportunity gap."[3]

As a counternarrative, this volume takes a look at some of the complexities of what it takes to support economically disadvantaged children to learn. Examining the issues through the eyes of teachers who are inside the urban teaching experience, we share the dilemmas they face in the midst of their many challenges and how they use their understanding of teaching and their communities to improve learning for the students in their care.

Our thinking in putting together this collection has been influenced greatly by perspectives emphasizing teachers as generators of knowledge who can inform practice, who are members of a profession, and who are potential agents of change. In contrast to the commonly held view of teachers as technicians, consumers, and receivers, who simply transmit information through curricula handed down from central offices, we offer, instead, a view of teachers as knowers and thinkers who can critique, challenge, and generate knowledge to contribute to improvements in schooling.[4]

ORGANIZATION AND METHODOLOGY OF THE BOOK

The stories we feature were selected from our review of over four hundred studies produced over the past decade by teacher-learners who have participated in the course on Inquiry Research that we teach at The City College of New York's School of Education. This two-semester culminating experience of our teacher preparation program provides participants with an opportunity to generate a personally meaningful teaching-related question, pursue the question by collecting and analyzing evidence, and use what they learn to inform their teaching. Ultimately, the teacher-learners produce a report that is both an account and an analysis of their work. Our purpose in engaging them in such a project is to instill in them the habit of asking and pursuing generative questions as an ongoing part of their professional lives. Through their personally meaningful explorations, teachers learn how to think critically, reflect on their work, connect theory with practice, take charge of their own learning, and take action to make change. By engaging in the nonlinear, and sometimes confusing, iterative cycle of inquiry—questions lead to other questions and evolve as they unfold—teacher-learners get a feel for what it means to be a questioner, a doer, and a knowledge maker; gain competence and confidence in their skills; learn how to articulate what they know; and, ultimately, translate the understanding gained from their own learning to the experiences they structure for their students.

Our aim in choosing the pieces presented here was not to showcase best practices or to highlight teachers who have all the answers, but rather to demonstrate how teachers' process of inquiring about their work leads them to learn and grow as professionals, ultimately benefiting the learning of their students. This is especially significant given that the teachers we work with—and so many others—grapple with challenges of urban settings (such as scripted curricula, high-stakes tests, students' challenging behaviors, families living with the stressors of economically disadvantaged neighborhoods, etc.) that many educators face but for which few strategies have been found to be effective.

As we sifted and sorted through our teacher colleagues' work, we identified four areas of concern that appeared repeatedly in their accounts: how to be responsive to cultural and linguistic diversity, how to differentiate instruction, how to establish effective home/school partnerships, and how to address the constraints of current educational policies and mandates. Selecting stories that exemplified each of these themes, we crafted narratives using the teachers' own words, incorporating their perspectives as best as we could. We based what we wrote on their writings, on conferences we had with them while engaged in their studies, and on interviews we held after they reviewed our drafts. (Almost all the names of the teacher-learners are their own, but names of the students they reference have been changed.)

In the resulting accounts, we try to maintain a careful balance between honoring the authenticity of the teachers' own words and shaping a contour for our own narrative. To accomplish this goal we read through their original reports, listening *for* their stories rather than *to* their stories, a distinction made by author Eudora Welty in her essays about her own writing.[5] While we did not compose or direct what teachers said as we wrote the ensuing chapters, we actively engaged in a dialogue with their dramas, searching for their central meanings, adjusting the rhythm and texture of their voices, seeking coherence for the overall work. We aimed to be the

> artist, painting the landscape, drawing their portraits, sketching in the light and the shadows . . . the probing researcher[s], patiently gathering data, asking the impertinent questions, examining their interpretations with skepticism and deliberation . . . the fellow traveler[s], walking beside them, watching their backs, admiring the vistas, avoiding the minefields, and bringing [our] own story to our dialogue.[6]

We recognize, however, that despite our best efforts to evoke these teachers' voices, in the end these stories are co-constructions. They are *our* tales of the teachers' learning.

In her seminal text *The Dreamkeepers: Successful Teachers of African American Children*, Gloria Ladson-Billings identified *respect*—for students, for their families, and for their cultures—as the fundamental trait of teachers who are effective at supporting the learning of African American children.[7] Respect is a salient feature that distinguishes the teachers in this book as well—respect not only for children and their communities but also for the process of teaching and learning. We are honored and deeply grateful that the teachers involved in this project have allowed us to shine a light on their work to reveal some of the untold stories from inside urban teaching. Within the details and nuances of their experiences, we believe, lie insights about issues and pressing problems that urban educators frequently face.

We share their accounts in the pages that follow in the hope that their investigations will illuminate the power of inquiry as a tool for professional learning and that their stories will foster new understanding and lead to much-needed improvements in schools.

Inside Culturally Responsive Teaching

What does it really mean to be a culturally responsive teacher of children from many different backgrounds and life experiences? What are the issues that teachers grapple with to address the challenges of this work? How do teachers' own personal backgrounds impact their efforts to support the children from diverse cultures who have been entrusted to their care?

In this section we share the work of four teachers who have all found effective yet distinctive ways to connect with the children and families in their classrooms in the diverse urban settings in which they teach. Some of these teachers are intimately familiar with what it means and feels like to be different, as they themselves come from backgrounds and/or have had life experiences that diverge from the dominant culture. As a result, they know firsthand what it means to feel like the other, to be ignored, or to be misunderstood. Adesina Abani,[1] an English-language learner from Nigeria who herself received little guidance from teachers as she acculturated to a new country, tells of how her own newcomer experience influenced her efforts to help a group of immigrant students negotiate their entry to school

7

in the United States. Beatrice Tinio, a Filipina American, describes having few memories from her many years of schooling in which the curriculum ever felt relevant to her. Likewise, Joleen Hanlon's account of her own experiences as a student grappling with her identity are memorable for the absence of any positive mention of differences in sexual orientation. In contrast, the story of Mary Williams describes being different from another vantage point. The challenges she faces as a white teacher who grew up in a well-resourced, homogeneous environment are depicted in her account of how she has struggled to transcend the privileges of her upbringing to find ways to be inclusive and responsive to the needs of students who are different from herself.

In the details and nuances of these teachers' actions we learn about teaching that respects and utilizes the rich yet often neglected resources of students' cultures, backgrounds, and experiences. The poignant stories of their work offer insights about some of the complexities involved in teaching diverse learners.

CHAPTER 1

Immigrant Children's Earliest Schooling Experiences: Adesina Abani

A desina Abani (pseudonym) remembers being excited to attend school in America when she migrated from Nigeria as a nine-year-old. She was especially glad to learn that teachers didn't hit students for misbehavior, as had been her experience in her country. Her high expectations, however, quickly faded as she began to experience life in her new school:

> I was a great student in Nigeria, so I couldn't wait to show off my skills here in the States. It was exciting with the new clothes, new supplies, everything, and then I got to school. I guess I had high hopes. It's just, I would say a month or two after it started, there were very few days when I can recall feeling happy in school. Very, very few days.

First she was teased about her accent. "That alone shut me down," she recollects. She figured out that, "if I don't say anything, I won't be teased." Although this strategy successfully avoided calling attention to her linguistic differences, Adesina experienced still other difficulties that she believes were caused by the fact that her background was different from that of others in her school. The most upsetting of these was when her teacher one day accused her of stealing from the classroom. Although her parents believed her when she went told them she was not guilty, Adesina was shaken by what she considered to be the teacher's unfair treatment. She barely slept as she relived her teacher's harsh words to her and awoke the morning after this incident filled with dread about the prospect of returning to school. When later the next day she discovered a classmate playing with the toy she had been accused of stealing, she told the teacher, but the teacher did nothing. Only when Adesina complained to the assistant principal was the accusation against her withdrawn. But her feelings of hurt lingered on. It wasn't until much later that Adesina came to realize these incidents were related to her immigrant status—how much the cultural differences between her and her classmates led to misunderstandings, misperceptions, and misjudgments about her.

Experiences like these from Adesina's childhood sensitized her to the challenges faced by other immigrant children: "As an immigrant, I know how scary being in a new country can be. It is important that the stress new immigrant children and their families are going through is taken into consideration when they set foot into a classroom." This insight was instrumental in Adesina's decision to select teaching as a career. She knows from experience how vital it is to school success to understand each child in the classroom: "I really try my best to reach out to my students. And I just feel like there is no way a child would be in my classroom and would just be sitting there and I wouldn't ask: Where are you from? What are you about? Tell me about your parents. Tell me about your siblings."

Adesina's desire to be a culturally responsive teacher led her to reach out to younger immigrant children to explore the issue of how best to teach them. To do this she launched a mentoring project with four children whom she met at her family's mosque. All of them had recently migrated to the United States: two brothers from Bangladesh—Habib and Kabir—who were eight and ten years old respectively; Mary from Nigeria, who was nine; and Sarah from Ghana, who was also nine. Through this work she developed an understanding of their perspectives and educational needs. As she engaged in individual and group conversations with the children and their families, along with observations of the children in school, Adesina gained insights about how she and other educators could support them as they transitioned to their new country and educational environment.

Even though Adesina had experienced schooling in a developing country, she was surprised to learn of the vast differences between the schooling the children and families had experienced in their countries of origin and the experiences they were having in U.S. schools.

SCHOOLING DIFFERENCES—PARENTS' PERSPECTIVES

From the parents of the children with whom Adesina worked, she learned of the scant resources that their countries of origin allotted to public education. By contrast, their perceptions of the public school their children attended in the United States were that it was well off, even though it was what many would consider to be an underresourced school compared to those in more affluent neighborhoods. They were pleased with what American public schools provide for free, especially in contrast to their own schooling experiences. Mary's mother noted that even "the most expensive [private] school in Nigeria is not as nice as my daughter's public school here in America." She explained that at the public school Mary attended in Nigeria, parents had to hire carpenters to have chairs and desks made for their children to use in school.

Habib's, Kabir's, and Sarah's parents all had similar experiences. The boys' father shared with Adesina that the public schools in Bangladesh were so overcrowded that he had selected to send his children to a private school. Yet even in this context he was required to pay extra for lunch and for all of their supplies and books. Sarah's mother had a similar experience. Although acknowledging that schooling in Ghana was changing in the direction of providing increased opportunities for the education of poor children, she described the schools as being underresourced, with parents having to purchase even the most basic supplies.

Adesina's conversations with these parents reminded her of the saying "One man's floor is another man's ceiling." It made her realize that although the conditions that she and her colleagues faced in the public schools of low-income communities in the United States were challenging, the problems (at least materially) seemed small compared to the issues raised by these parents. She was humbled: "I can't help but think how fortunate we are in this country that our children can attend school for free without worrying about what they will sit on to learn or if they will be able to eat at school."

It wasn't until some time later, when Adesina made a return visit to Nigeria, that she understood, through her adult eyes, the portrait of educational life in the developing world that the parents in her project had shared with her. When she visited her cousin's Nigerian middle school she learned that having sixty students in a classroom with only one teacher was quite common. Adesina was astonished: "The teacher didn't even know who his own students were. There were that many! The students who grabbed his attention were his superstudents. If you didn't sit within the first few rows and you weren't actively participating in class, you faded away. A lot of children did not get the attention they needed. If there were ever a classroom like this [in America], every single civil rights group would be so irate and surrounding that school, protesting."

SCHOOLING DIFFERENCES—
CHILDREN'S PERSPECTIVES

Like their parents, the four children in Adesina's project were excited about the advantages offered by their new New York City school, especially the opportunities afforded to them that seemed so extravagant compared to the inadequate resources of the schools in their home countries. They were particularly delighted about having classes in physical education, computer, library, and music. Recalling the first time she went to music class, Mary described her surprise to find that "there were keyboards and we all were able to touch and play on them. It was so exciting. I had never touched a keyboard before." Likewise, Sarah shared her sense of awe when she attended her first dance class. She said "the room was so big, bigger than my class, and the teacher played different music and we all danced. It was so much fun. The dance teacher is starting a cheerleading team and I am going to try out." Gym was Kabir's favorite class. He explained, "I love playing basketball. We don't even have to fight for a ball because everybody has their own." And Habib added, "I love the art studio. There are all kinds of arts stuff and we make really cool projects. I had never seen some of the art materials before."

Another point of excitement for the children about schooling in the United States was the opportunity they had during the school day for field trips. "I never went on a field trip during school in Nigeria. Trips are so much fun," said Mary. Habib added, "I love that we get to move around," and explained that his class would soon be visiting a museum in Brooklyn. He was especially excited about the prospect of this trip because he had never been to a museum before.

As she listened to the children talk so excitedly and happily about their new experiences, Adesina was surprised at first by the ease with which her young mentees were adapting to their new circumstances and the lack of problems they were experiencing. They were having very different experiences than she had had as a child. But then she realized all of the advantages they have that she did not have as a new immigrant. First of all, they had *her* as a mentor. Adesina met with them at the mosque three or four times a week, listening to them talk about their school days, helping them and their parents negotiate cultural differences and other adjustments to their new land. Second, these kids were not the sole immigrants in their school, as had been the case with Adesina many years ago. Minorities today, many of whom are immigrants, make up more than 40 percent of New York City's population, clustered heavily in neighborhoods like Adesina's, where they find others with similar experiences.[2]

And finally, Adesina realized that an understanding about what is effective teaching is more present in the schools today than when Adesina was a child. The classrooms attended by the kids in Adesina's project were not the teacher-focused, "chalk and talk" classrooms of yesteryear, organized into rows of desks with the teacher at the front doling out information that the students were expected to silently digest and spew out. Instead they feature students grouped together at tables and chairs, animatedly engrossed in conversations as they engage in projects and other active learning experiences. Teachers are also more aware of the need to use children's backgrounds as resources for learning. For instance, when Sarah's class studied Africa, the teacher made sure to include Ghana, Sarah's homeland, as one of the countries they explored, asking Sarah to share her early memories from there. Adesina was pleased to learn how much more diverse school populations are today than they were in her childhood, and how much more the classroom experience provides opportunities for children from different backgrounds to feel included.

CULTURAL CLASHES—BIG AND SMALL

Although Adesina did not find the big challenges she had anticipated in the immigrant children's experiences—such as problems with learning a new language or coping with overt prejudice—she found herself dealing with issues that at first seemed mundane but that actually loomed large in the children's eyes.

Food

Food was a "biggy"; the children were trying to get used to the strange American food. All four of the children in her project were accustomed to home-cooked traditional food from their countries. They hated the food from their school's cafeteria. Once, while observing Kabir in the cafeteria, Adesina noticed that he ate an apple and some vegetables, drank his milk, and, after sniffing his pizza, made a disgusted expression. He proceeded to dump his tray's contents in the garbage. Later she watched Sarah, Mary, and Habib react to their pizza in similar ways. When Adesina asked the children about their preferences, they eagerly shared more about what foods they disliked. Sarah said that "all that gooey stuff looks nasty." Kabir reported that they "served this stick thing and it has cheese inside. I did not like it." Habib complained that the pizza was "too greasy." All of them agreed that they would rather spend the afternoon hungry than eat most of what the cafeteria served for lunch. The only food that they all liked was peanut butter and jelly sandwiches.

Adesina related the children's experiences with school food to her own childhood experiences. Remembering when her family first migrated to the United States, she recalled going out to eat at McDonald's. Each time they went, her father would buy apple pies for dessert. He would encourage Adesina to taste the pie, but she didn't like it and would always spit it right out. She could not understand why anyone would want to bake apples! No one in her country ever did this. "It just did not make sense to me," she said. It took a while, but eventually she developed a taste for apple pie.

Propelled by her own memories of adjusting to American food, as well as by the children's stories about their school food experiences, Adesina arranged a meeting with the school's principal to advocate for having more choices made available for them at school meals. After explaining to the principal her own past and the children's current reluctance to embrace "foreign" foods, she raised the possibility of making the peanut butter and jelly sandwiches that the children liked available as a daily alternative to school lunch. In response, the principal spoke to the lunchroom director and they acted on Adesina's suggestion. Pleased with the new arrangement, the children—together with Adesina—made a big thank-you card for the principal and the lunchroom director.

Legal Issues

A tremendous stressor for immigrant families is the difficulty of obtaining a green card allowing one to legally work in the United States. This stress likely affects immigrant children indirectly in ways that may not be easy to identify or articulate. Adesina had firsthand experience with this kind of stress. When she was in high school, her guidance counselor applied for a scholarship for her, which she won, that would have paid for a part of her college tuition. However, she was not able to take advantage of this opportunity because she did not have a green card. While her parents had successfully secured their own legal status, the process had been so lengthy and expensive that they had not yet been able to save enough money to apply for cards for their children. So Adesina lost her scholarship along with numerous employment opportunities. By the time she finally received her registration number, she was in her final semester of college.

Immigration status was an issue of concern for every family in Adesina's project. Only one parent, Mr. Ahmad, was close to receiving his registration number. In the meantime, he earned minimum wage working for a friend who paid him "off the books." The parents of the other three children were also not able to work legally in this country. Being unable to adequately care for their families caused them great pain. Mary's mom tearfully admitted, "I am currently here on a visa. I wanted to stay and that is why I enrolled my daughter in school, but I can't get a job. . . . I can't make a life for myself because I don't have a green card. I am thinking of going back to Nigeria. There I have family and I can return back to my old job." Sarah's mom, who relied on her savings and an off-the-books job in order to survive, added, "I feel the same way. At least in Ghana I know my way around. I can do little odd jobs to make money, but here every job requires a green card. I came to America because I thought things would be easier but I feel like a hungry dog and someone is dangling a big piece of meat in front of me and I can't get to it."

During the course of Adesina's project, Mary and her mother did subsequently return to Nigeria. The process of obtaining a green card proved too expensive for them to continue. "We both cried when she told me she was leaving," said Adesina. "I wanted so badly to encourage her to stay, but the truth was, that would have been unfair. She couldn't work, her savings were running out, and her frustration was leading to a deep depression. . . . I still feel the pain of saying good-bye to them." This dilemma brought home to Adesina how fortunate she was that her own family had been successful at achieving legal resident status so that they were able to make sure she had everything that she needed. Many immigrants, she realized, have no one to turn to. "Eventually . . . you go through your savings [and] homelessness is your next stop." These experiences that Adesina had with her mentees helped her to understand in a new and profound way that in order for teachers to be able to help their students, they needed to help their students' parents as well.

Parent Involvement

In many countries, schools are viewed as the realm solely of teachers; parent involvement is frowned upon as interference. The parents of the children in Adesina's project brought this attitude about parent involvement with them to their children's school. They had no expectation of getting involved. In the United States, however, parent involvement is seen as a critical element of academic success. Adesina quickly came to realize that in order for teachers to help immigrant children in school, they need to explain this different perspective to parents and encourage them to get involved in their children's schooling. Adesina made an effort to do this with the parents of the children in her project. As a result of her guidance, she experienced some success: Habib and Kabir's mother began contacting her children's teachers and volunteering at their school. She even became the recording secretary for the PTA. Sarah's mother also got involved by baking for the school's bake sale, which raised funds to buy new instruments for the school's music program.

THE LEARNING CONTINUES

Adesina's project, originally intended as a time-limited exploration of how teachers can provide support to enhance immigrant children's learning, actually has not come to an end. Although several years have passed since the project's inception, Adesina is still in contact with the families, all of whom have become active participants in their children's lives and schools. The children, now doing well in middle school, are still in contact with Adesina, who continues to serve as their mentor. What she has learned the most from her experiences is that social issues play a big role in academics: "If you are not comfortable with who you are then you are not going to be comfortable sharing who you are with other people."

The job for teachers, Adesina has learned, is to ensure that all children can bring their authentic selves to school, have the realities of their lives acknowledged, feel safe and supported to address their challenges, and use their cultural resources as a foundation to maximize learning opportunities. Such an approach will benefit not just immigrant children but all children who attend our nation's schools. The message they will see modeled is that diverse experiences and perspectives offer rich possibilities for learning.

Ideas from Inside Adesina's Classroom

♦ The difficulties of obtaining a green card to be able to legally work in the United States can be a tremendous stressor in the lives of families new to the United States, and this stress can negatively impact their children.

♦ The social life of children plays an important role in their learning. If children feel welcomed and are encouraged to share their history in the classroom, they will more likely feel at ease to be themselves, ask questions, and take the risks required for genuine learning.

♦ A mentor who understands the process of becoming acclimated to the culture and customs of a new country can be a helpful resource for newly immigrated children.

♦ Utilizing the cultural resources and experiences of immigrant children can support their learning while also broadening perspectives for all children, helping them to respect and value differences.

CHAPTER 2

Celebrating Diversity in the Classroom: Beatrice Tinio

Beatrice Tinio is a Filipina American who, as a child, attended a predominantly white elementary school. Often feeling like an outsider in this environment, she longed to be and look like everyone else. "I remember wishing my mother would pack me a 'normal' lunch," she recalls, "so nobody would have to ask me what it was I was eating." Besides recollecting feelings like these, Beatrice can locate few memories of school in which the learning felt relevant to her. She explains: "I do not remember learning about leaders or historical figures that I could connect with. Our school had one day out of the year to celebrate different customs—"International Food Day"—where children were required to bring in a traditional dish from their cultural heritage. I always thought, why should this be only one day out of the year? We should be learning and inquiring about each other's backgrounds daily."

This disconnect between school and Beatrice's reality lasted through her adolescence. Looking back now, she sees it as a key factor in difficulties she experienced in developing relationships with teachers and other peers.

It wasn't until she was well into college, where she was among a more diverse population and able to select courses of interest to her, that she began to feel more comfortable in her own skin and find relevance in what she learned in school.

Now a second grade teacher in her thirties, Beatrice has taught for several years in a public charter school in the South Bronx, a low-income neighborhood of New York City that is home mostly to Hispanic and black Americans. The majority of the children in her class qualify for free or reduced lunch and over half of them come from families who speak a language at home that is not English. Despite this diversity of her students, however, the required curriculum offers little that connects to the children's backgrounds. Recognizing a striking parallel between what she has to teach in her current setting and what she experienced in her own childhood schooling, and motivated by the memories of her feelings of invisibility when she herself was a student, Beatrice is dedicated to finding ways to bring the perspectives of diverse languages, cultures, races, and religions into her classroom:

> I listen, observe, and have rich discussions with my students based on their inquiries and ideas about people who are different than they are. I see the children's curiosity level rise when other children talk about why Kelary doesn't stand up for the Pledge of Allegiance, or why Seidina isn't from Africa even though he's black. These issues and social concerns within my classroom are very important to me as a teacher, as a human being, and should be incorporated into our daily discussions and teachings. I am aware that school is one of the many vast concentric circles that affect children's lives, and I believe that our social and emotional behaviors are impacted greatly by our interactions with our classmates and teachers. I hope that I can provide my students with richer knowledge and dialogue about concepts that they are unaware of which may give them a

greater appreciation and recognition of people's differences and similarities.

To help her work on these goals, Beatrice decided to explore how she could infuse diverse perspectives into her curriculum. Her intent was to learn how doing this could help her to promote positive behaviors among the students as well as help them to feel good about themselves.

Seeking background information for her study, Beatrice read a lot about multicultural education and interviewed several experienced teachers who seemed to be doing a good job of creating an inclusive atmosphere in their classrooms. Additionally, she tried out different teaching strategies, documenting—through journal entries, photographs, and samples of students' work—what she was trying and how her efforts were impacting her students.

Regularly she reviewed the information she was collecting, using it to shape and guide subsequent teaching. This ongoing process of research and reflection helped her throughout the course of the school year to better understand how her students were learning, what in her teaching was going well, and what areas of work she needed to strengthen to become a more effective, inclusive educator.

TRYING OUT IDEAS IN THE CLASSROOM

Beatrice's efforts to become a more culturally responsive teacher focused on two areas: (1) presenting the children with experiences, materials, and ideas that exposed them to other countries and cultures; and (2) creating an atmosphere in her classroom of acceptance and respect. What follows are some examples of what she did.

Exposing Children to the Diverse World

To begin, Beatrice used every opportunity she could to bring the world into her classroom. She provisioned her reading center with literature about different countries and cultures; created an artifact center that displayed objects, instruments, and fabrics representing many parts of the globe; played music in the listening center from faraway places; displayed in the computer center videos of dances from Russia, Nigeria, and other countries; and developed a slide-show center where children were able to look at the architecture of distant localities.

While much of what Beatrice brought into the classroom was not a part of the official curriculum, she found ways to use these culturally relevant materials to teach to the city and state standards. Consciously integrating required knowledge and skills into activities and assignments, she replaced didactic lessons and fill-in-the-blank worksheets with interesting questions, rich discussions, and projects that integrated the disciplines. Beatrice soon noticed how much more her students enjoyed learning from these rich, active contexts than they did from completing the textbook tasks that had dominated their class work in prior grades. Inspired, she continued her experimentation.

Connecting to Children's Cultural Backgrounds

Quickly, it became evident to Beatrice that children are eager to share personal experiences when they engage in an activity, lesson, or story that connects to them and their culture. This spurs them to talk with and learn from each other. She recounts an example:

One morning, I read a book about [the holiday] Ramadan. That whole week prior I had read books that represented different cultural holidays and celebrations. Before I could even finish the book, one boy in my class, Sayid, shouted out that he knew of several mosques around New York. I asked him how he knew this and he proceeded to tell me that his family is Muslim. He seemed quite enthusiastic and eager to speak more about this holiday and his religion. He elaborated on some of the details in the book and answered questions asked by other students. One child asked him, "What is Eid?" Sayid replied, "Eid is a special holiday that comes at the end of Ramadan and there is a special hug that is done. Can I show you, Ms. Tinio?" I nodded my approval and he demonstrated with me to the class. He put both of his hands on my shoulders and he told me to do the same to him. At shoulder length apart we drew each other closer, our shoulders touching once on the left side, once on the right side, and back again to the left side.

Although he had been in my classroom for four months, I did not know until then that he was Muslim. Until that moment, he or his parents never spoke about it with me. But now, he seemed to be very proud. I felt more of a connection with him knowing this and acknowledging it. Embracing him in that way drew me closer to him as a whole child.

This experience, which gave Beatrice and the other students in the class rich information about Sayid, was made possible only because she had recognized and included his culture in the classroom. As a result, he proudly shared his knowledge. His response is testimony to students' willingness to open up to their teachers and peers when they feel they are in an environment that welcomes individuals from different backgrounds.

Sayid's willingness to share himself proved to be contagious. Other students also responded to Beatrice's efforts to infuse literature, art, and ideas of other cultures into the curriculum of the class. The poem in Figure 1 is an example, composed by one of Beatrice's students after the class read a book about personal identity. In her writing, the child shares her heritage as well as her worries, hopes, and dreams.

LISTENING TO CHILDREN'S VOICES

When teachers provide opportunities for children to engage in activities to which they personally can connect, children get interested and involved.

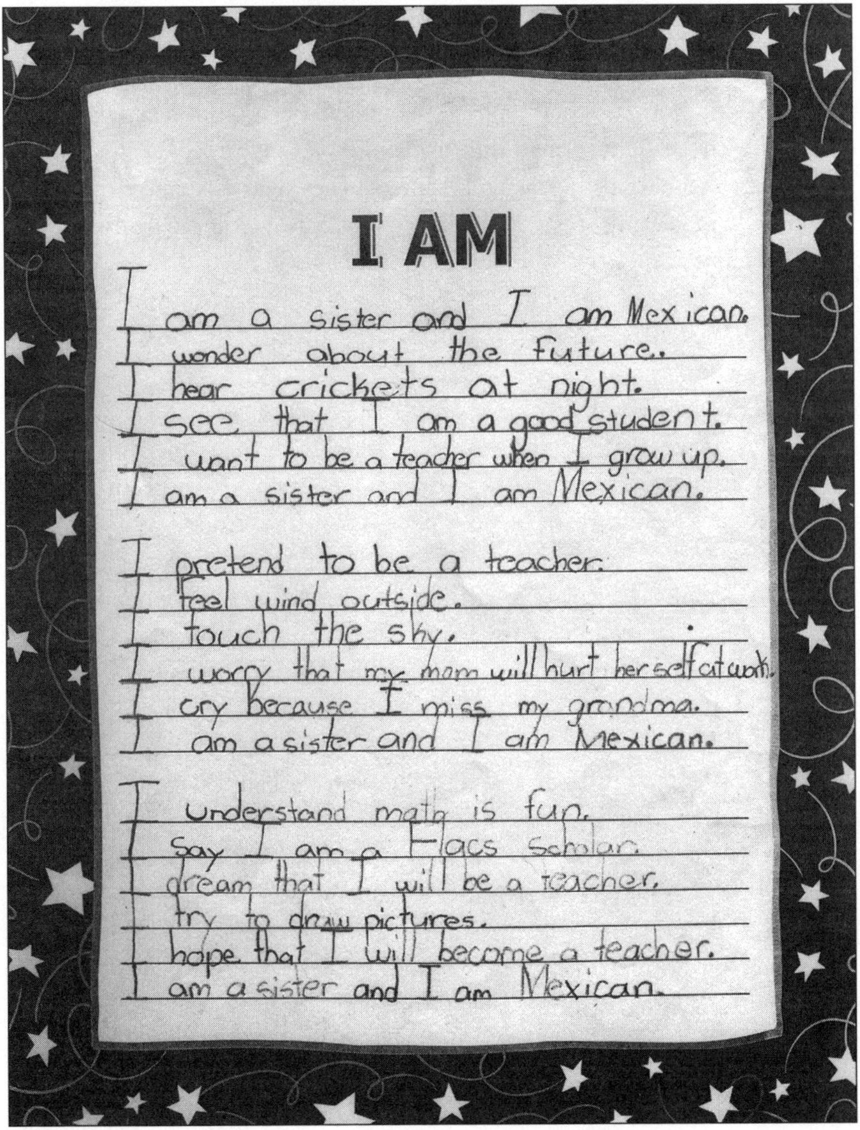

I AM

I am a sister and I am Mexican.
I wonder about the future.
I hear crickets at night.
I see that I am a good student.
I want to be a teacher when I grow up.
I am a sister and I am Mexican.

I pretend to be a teacher.
I feel wind outside.
I touch the sky.
I worry that my mom will hurt herself at work.
I cry because I miss my grandma.
I am a sister and I am Mexican.

I understand math is fun.
I say I am a Flacs scholar.
I dream that I will be a teacher.
I try to draw pictures.
I hope that I will become a teacher.
I am a sister and I am Mexican.

Figure 1.

As a result, lively conversations take place. And when teachers then take the time to listen and respond to this talk, it becomes possible for valuable learning—for both teachers and students—to occur. Because what children say offers insight to who they are and how they process information, teachers can take what they learn from what they hear to shape curriculum and enhance teaching strategies. In this way, a learning environment can develop that is responsive to children's interests and needs.

Beatrice became aware of how this process takes place by observing a visiting teaching artist at work in her classroom. Beatrice explains:

> Since my class was learning about different countries and cultures, Lauren, the visiting teaching artist, worked with the students to create different instruments from different countries. In the process, one student, Tyler, recognized a percussion instrument and said to his three tablemates, "I have that same thing in my culture." Angel asked, "Where have you seen this before?" Tyler responded, "In St. Lucia, where my mother is from." Flora, another one of his tablemates, asked, "Where is St. Lucia?" Tyler replied, "It's near Puerto Rico and it's an island."

Beatrice noted what Tyler said and then later asked Tyler to share with the whole class what she had overheard him tell the others at his table. She showed the children where St. Lucia and Puerto Rico are on the map. Of course, this spurred other children to share their families' countries of origin and to find these countries on the classroom's map. Then she asked more questions about the guiro, the percussion instrument Tyler recognized from his country of St. Lucia. Other children responded to Tyler's information by volunteering examples of instruments that are part of their families' cultures. Tyler's confidence about his knowledge and pride in his heritage was evident as he gave everyone more information about his background. In response, the other children in the class learned from him and became interested in a new place about which they had had little previous knowledge.

Offering opportunities for children to learn through and with their peers in this way promotes their interest in what others have to say. This helps to establish a culture in the class that values each and every member. And when regular opportunities are provided to practice behaviors such as these, children increasingly feel important, strengthening feelings of safety and acceptance, thus enhancing relationships in the classroom and beyond.

DEVELOPING STRATEGIES FOR PROBLEM SOLVING

Learning to solve problems and deal with tough issues is an important part of living in a diverse world. When children communicate with each other and process issues that reflect who they are and the world in which they live, they begin to acquire the kind of thinking skills needed for successful problem solving. In her efforts to become a more culturally responsive teacher, Beatrice consciously tried to teach these skills to her students to help them prepare for life's daily challenges. Her goal was to nurture strategies and communication skills for coping, making choices, and transforming negative situations into positive ones. The following story, told in Beatrice's words, illustrates how she went about this:

One afternoon Sayid complained to me that his good friend Alan made fun of him during lunch and he didn't understand why. Since this was the first time I'd heard of them not getting along, I asked Sayid if he felt comfortable speaking to Alan himself, with me present. Sayid agreed and we proceeded to have a conference. He asked Alan why he called him names and then Alan looked at me and said, "My mom does not want me to be friends with him. And during lunchtime my sister watches me and then she'll tell my mom." I asked

Alan if he enjoys being friends with Sayid. He said yes. In my mind I am thinking this is a racial issue because Sayid is an African American Muslim and Alan is Mexican. Whether this was a wrong accusation on my part or not, that's what I thought and I was wondering what to do next. So I asked the both of them what could we do to solve this problem? How could the two remain friends with Alan's mom accepting it? The boys first thought of speaking to Alan's mother. I advised that she might not feel comfortable talking about it in front of people other than her son. I asked them if they could think of another way to let her know they want to be friends without speaking to her directly. That is when Sayid suggested writing her a letter. I agreed, Alan agreed, and I told them that I would be happy to help them write it if they needed me to. I would also get it translated into Spanish for them. They looked relieved, happy, and proud of the solution they came up with.

I thought it was amazing that Alan, who has limited English language skills, was able to let me know about his mother. He was honest and upfront and I could see that he was genuinely disturbed by the situation. I was happy that both boys felt comfortable enough to talk about their feelings. The issues they raised are challenging to talk about and explore. I admit it wasn't easy for me to talk about either. But giving them the opportunity to share their fears and to work it out will hopefully support their social and problem-solving skills as adults.

Beatrice skillfully used the conflict just described to teach the children to listen to each other, appreciate each other's perspectives, and to think carefully about how to work together towards solving a very complicated problem. What she did helped the children involved—and all the others who were watching as well—feel safe, listened to, accepted for their differences, and represented in some way.

BUILDING COMMUNITY IN THE CLASSROOM

Beatrice's stories demonstrate how her responsiveness to the children and their different backgrounds built a sense of community in the classroom. To affirm and celebrate it, she launched a project to culminate the school year: the creation of a class quilt that would symbolize and reinforce all of the qualities she had been trying to instill in the children throughout the year.

To begin, she had the children create different patterns from various pieces of fabric—some that she provided for them and some that were provided by their families to represent the cultures or significant aspects of the children's lives. The children used these materials, working together in small groups, each gluing his or her individual design onto a square. When these were completed, Beatrice sewed the squares together in sections that represented the groups in which the children had worked. These squares became the top part of the quilt, which Beatrice then backed and finished off.

The process of making the quilt was a lot of fun, consolidating connections and trust among the children—exactly the feelings that Beatrice had worked so hard to nurture in them throughout the year. Beatrice's reflection on the final product expresses what she hoped to accomplish from the project: "With this quilt, each child's visual voice is represented. It is my duty as a teacher to connect and thread together these diverse pieces onto the larger fabric of society. Although each child's ideas and opinions are valued, it is also my job to help guide them toward a common goal."

EXPANDED VISIONS, SURPRISES, AND OTHER CONCLUDING THOUGHTS

Prior to embarking on this project to find ways to become a more culturally responsive teacher, Beatrice was worried about how she would be able to include multicultural education in the context of her school's required

Figure 2. Created by all the students of class 221 in Family Life Academy Charter School, Beatrice Tinio, Christina Pablo, and Marge Mendel, 2009–2010 school year.

curriculum. But as she dove deeper into the work, she realized that culturally responsive teaching need not be a "program" or prescribed set of lessons. Rather, she came to understand that educating about diversity is a process—of understanding different perspectives and of recognizing that these differences are shaped by many aspects of our society.

Effective culturally responsive teaching, Beatrice concluded, is both teaching *about* different cultures and teaching *to* different cultures. It involves using literature, visuals, artifacts, art, and music from many different cultures to shape and enrich *all* areas of study so that *all* students can see that they are represented. This kind of teaching needs to be infused in *all* curricula (whether the curricula are mandated or not), going beyond a focus on the content of what is taught to a focus on including diverse students, validating each person, ensuring that each person's voice is heard, nurturing awareness of and curiosity about others, learning to respect others' perspectives, and finding a way to balance how to be an individual in a group.[3] Beatrice's reflections on this newly developed understanding differ from her earlier thinking:

> When looking [for] and learning ways of how to implement a more diverse curriculum within a rigid one, I thought it would be problematic. I was looking for a clear method that I thought would be challenging to incorporate. But after reading about other approaches that concentrate on developing awareness, respect, acceptance, and providing equal opportunities, I realized that I had already been practicing this in my classroom. I just needed to consciously plan out and patch concepts together in order to address certain needs of my students. Once I was able to balance what was required of me from administration and the ideas of multiculturalism, it was easier and much more engaging and fun than I thought it ever could be. I've come to understand that as long as I maintain this stance toward the children, I can teach almost anything and be not only respectful of but responsive to their diversity as well.

Although much of what Beatrice learned through her study confirmed many of her ideas and past practices, she also discovered, to her surprise, that her efforts to be a more culturally responsive teacher actually supported her students in more ways than she had expected. With pleasure she noticed that the experiences she was providing for them helped to strengthen their academic skills—in reading, writing, and in math. And with delight she also noticed increased development in their problem-solving skills. But what struck her most deeply was the personal, transformational impact of her work:

> I expected some level of effect on the children, but not quite as deep and complex as what I found during this research. (It is interesting what you see and hear in a classroom when you give yourself that chance to look and seek out patterns.) What I learned is that encouraging children to share their cultural backgrounds makes them feel valued and appreciated as individuals and as a group. They gain greater self-awareness as well as a heightened empathy and understanding for each other.

As with most things in life, a careful examination reveals more complexity than previously imagined. Beatrice's study is a case in point. While confirming her understandings that originated in her experiences as an "outsider" in the homogenous school of her childhood, it also provided her with strategies for how to use these understandings to help nurture young citizens who can, hopefully, create a more generous community in our increasingly diverse world.

Beatrice sums up her expanded vision of teaching and her goals for the future in the following statement written for an exhibition of her class quilt:

> The standard definition of [quilting] is "to sew up between pieces of material," and I believe that is what I do everyday in teaching, finding ways to piece voices together, seeking connections, and establishing a common goal. At times it is challenging to stitch together

and find a connection between one view [and] another, but a thread is there. It is just about working through the thickness of the fabric to close up the gap.

In many cultures, quilts tell a story, usually about a family's history. Our quilt tells a story about how all individuals have a valued voice, and how those voices connect to the larger fabric of society. The story includes all 27 children in my second grade class who created patterns that represent who they are in that moment of making it. These patterns were patched together imperfectly to capture the essence of [what] we all are, human. I want this quilt to symbolize the mixing and intermingling of different shapes, colors, sizes, patterns, like ourselves, and how they all can be seen harmoniously living together.

Ideas from Inside Beatrice's Classroom

♦ Encouraging children to share their cultural backgrounds makes them feel valued and appreciated as individuals with interesting histories and backgrounds. They gain greater self-awareness as well as a heightened empathy and understanding for each other.

♦ Classroom conflicts can be used as opportunities to teach children to listen to each other and appreciate each others' perspectives.

♦ Culturally responsive teaching goes beyond a focus on the content of what is taught to a focus on including diverse students, validating who each person is, ensuring that each person's voice is heard, nurturing awareness of and curiosity about others, learning to respect others' perspectives, and finding a way to balance how to be an individual in a group.

♦ When children feel represented in the content of what they are being taught, they can be motivated to do better academically.

♦ Effective culturally responsive teaching is both teaching *about* different cultures and teaching *to* different cultures. It is not a "program" or prescribed curriculum. Rather, it involves infusing into *all* curricula the literature, visuals, artifacts, art, and music from many different cultures to shape and enrich *all* areas of study so that *all* students can see that they are represented and come to understand the different perspectives represented in many aspects of our society.

CHAPTER 3

Breaking the Silence—Countering Homophobia in Schools: Joleen Hanlon

According to a survey by the Gay, Lesbian, and Straight Education (GLSEN) Network, nearly nine out of ten lesbian, gay, bisexual, and transgender (LGBT) students experience harassment at school and nearly two-thirds feel unsafe because of their sexual orientation. Almost a third of LGBT students skip at least one day of school each month because of these concerns.[4] Victims of homophobic bullying and/or violence are at risk for suicide, depression, abusing drugs, engaging in unsafe sex, and becoming homeless.[5] In fact, gay teens are four times more likely than straight teens to attempt suicide.[6]

These alarming statistics motivated Joleen Hanlon, a new-to-the-profession teacher, to devote herself to making schools safer and more comfortable for young people identifying as lesbian, gay, bisexual, or transgender. Remembering her own struggle with gender identity as a youth, she believes it is vitally important for children in schools to be provided with opportunities to explore their understanding of sexual orientation issues: "I can still remember the first and only time one of my teachers referred to a lesbian. It was amazing to hear a teacher validate the existence of gay people in a positive context. This sent an important message to me at a time when I only heard gay people discussed in a derogatory manner."

Now, years later, as an adult, Joleen has observed that homophobia is still prevalent in schools and is concerned that teachers do little to address it. An incident she witnessed while doing fieldwork in a school as part of her teacher education program offers an example:

> The boys were looking at wrestling cards, and one of the boys was really excited about this one male wrestler. And the friends around him were grossed out that he really loved that wrestler and called him "gay." They said it pretty loud and I thought the teacher could have heard, but she didn't respond. So at the end of class I mentioned it to her that they were making fun of him and that he seemed pretty upset. And she said they always do that kind of thing and said there's nothing she can do, and shrugged it off. It made me think more, and I wondered, Why are teachers afraid to talk about it, and why isn't it in the curriculum?

In an effort to find answers to this question, Joleen launched an investigation into how differences in gender and sexual orientation are handled in school, how homophobia is manifested, and how to break the silence about it that is so hurtful to so many children. She interviewed nine educators and observed many children in classrooms in four different New York City schools.

GENDER NORMS AND HOMOPHOBIA

Joleen began her study by observing how narrow definitions of what it means to be male or female lead to homophobia—the fear or hatred of lesbian, gay, bisexual, or transgendered people. In one second grade classroom she noticed children regularly using "the G word" (gay) in negative and taunting ways. When Joleen questioned Jade about why she called Adam "gay," the child explained that she called Adam "gay" because he liked Hannah Montana. When Joleen asked her what "gay" meant, Jade explained to her that it was when a boy likes "girl things" and a girl likes "boy things," and, to Jade, this was bad.

Such strict gender definitions, Joleen also noticed, were often reinforced (although perhaps unintentionally) by teachers' actions in the classroom. One example is the common school practice of separating children by gender—into boys' and girls' lines. Joleen observed that "this can create a problem for students who do not fully identify with their birth-assigned sex." This was the case for Shauna, a third grader who identified as a girl but often enjoyed socializing with boys, playing softball, and wearing loose, masculine clothing. Occasionally, Shauna chose to stay in the boys' line at line-up time, in spite of the fact that doing this resulted in her being taunted by other children. Fortunately, she had a teacher who allowed her to go to and stay in any line that she chose. But this teacher did little to address the other children's taunting. Why should this child "have to risk ridicule and break a class routine in order to assert her identity?" questioned Joleen. "Boys' and girls' lines may be convenient for teachers, but that doesn't mean they are necessarily good for each child."

Not all children negotiate these identity issues as easily as Shauna, Joleen noted from other observations. Kara, who socialized mostly with boys and dressed like a boy, was continually harassed and questioned about her gender by others in her class and school. Kara's teacher noted that boys from the class would pick on her and ask her, "Are you a boy or a girl? Why do you look like a boy when you're a girl?" Kara even faced humiliation from adults at the school. A staff member, once finding her in the girls' bathroom and assuming that she was a boy, yelled at Kara to get out. Another teacher was overheard wondering aloud, in front of a group of children, if Kara was a girl or a boy.

Situations such as Jade's, Shauna's, and Kara's called Joleen's attention "to the need for teachers to be aware of gender issues and of how our strict gender expectations can negatively affect children in subtle yet profound ways." She was becoming more and more convinced that if educators better understood gender identity and sexual orientation, they could help to prevent discrimination and better support all children to grow.

TEACHERS' DISCOMFORT

Curious to learn more about educators' responses to gender-related issues, Joleen interviewed teachers and administrators, asking them to describe situations in which they responded to homophobic attitudes. She found that the nature of these educators' responses was directly connected to their level of discomfort about the issues. Most of the teachers Joleen interviewed admitted to being uncomfortable talking about LGBT issues and, because of this, either ignored homophobic behavior or just minimally addressed it. In contrast, those who were more comfortable used the discriminatory incidents that they regularly encountered as opportunities to educate and teach about being part of a caring community.

The connection between teachers' comfort level and self-censorship became clearer to Joleen when she began work as an assistant teacher. The lead teacher in her classroom was uncomfortable about discussing with the children any topic that was related to same-sex relationships. The teacher was even reluctant to have Joleen or anyone read the children a book that depicted families who had different configurations. This really disturbed Joleen. She wondered, How would a child who had two moms or two dads or perhaps a relative who was gay feel about not seeing or hearing about her reality reflected in conversations or in books? Once again Joleen realized that she was in a context where a teacher's silence had the potential to marginalize or exclude a child.

Other teachers whom Joleen interviewed also expressed a reluctance to address variations in sexual orientation. Some, even those who themselves were accepting of differences in their personal lives, were afraid to do anything to offend anyone in school. Others feared that their untenured status as an employee might be jeopardized if they raised "controversial" issues. One first-year teacher told Joleen that "it really should be part of the curriculum. Absolutely! The more that it's talked about, the more it becomes the norm and the less stigma it will have." However, this teacher did not act on her beliefs. "I'm going to be honest," she shared with Joleen. "I'm a first-year teacher and a lot of things make me nervous." She reminded Joleen of past precedents where individuals were punished for their beliefs:[7] In the 1990s the chancellor of the New York City public schools had been brought down because of strong parental and organizational opposition to his introduction of a curriculum that promoted tolerance of differences (including homosexuality) through such suggested readings as *Daddy's Roommate*[8] and *Heather Has Two Mommies.*[9]

Despite the overwhelming reluctance Joleen encountered about speaking up about controversial issues, she *did* find a few veteran teachers who offered suggestions for how to acknowledge and support variations in gender and sexual orientation. One argued that there's no reason to exclude LGBT people if we are preparing children to live in a society that's diverse: "To leave them out seems like we have our own biases." Another explained that she responds to her students' antigay language because she sees it as comparable to racist attitudes. "How is calling someone gay in a negative way different than using a racial slur?" she would ask them upon hearing such talk. She reminded them, "We are all people first and we need to remember that."

It seemed to Joleen that it was no accident that both of these teachers had job security and were working in schools where the administration was active in combating discrimination. These facts strengthened Joleen's conviction that schoolwide professional development needs to include education about all kinds of diversity.

SHATTERING TABOOS ONE STEP AT A TIME

As a result of Joleen's investigation of how schools address differences in gender and sexual orientation and how they respond to homophobia, her convictions have been strengthened about the need for schools to create safe, inclusive environments. Breaking the silence about homophobia, she believes, is a key ingredient to making this happen.

Now that she is a second grade teacher working in an urban public school, Joleen continues her efforts to put her values into practice. She is not afraid to explore children's reactions to differences and tries to model, at every opportunity, openness and acceptance to all. For example, when a girl in her class was teased about her facial hair, Joleen explained to the children that different cultures have different perceptions of beauty. In contrast to images of beauty in our country, some cultures, she explained, consider dark hair (between women's eyes, above their lips, on their arms and legs) to be the ideal. She showed the class pictures of the artist Frida Kahlo, who exemplifies this image of beauty. In addition to challenging the children's conception of what is beautiful, Kahlo's photos also challenged their notions of what is feminine, because Kahlo frequently dressed in masculine clothing. By taking on this issue, Joleen gained confidence in her abilities to take advantage of other "teachable moments" regarding differences that regularly arise in the classroom.

In small ways like these Joleen has pursued her aim of breaking the silence about homophobia and other forms of discrimination. Joleen's efforts also include writing articles about these issues, which she has subsequently shared with her colleagues. Additionally, she has raised issues of diversity at schoolwide meetings, which has led the school's administration to offer a workshop on bullying and to support the formation of a schoolwide action research project focused on observing and documenting sources of conflict among children. Joleen is hopeful that this work will lead to openings for discussion of still other controversial subjects. She is especially pleased to note that just recently the school mandated that children no longer be separated into boy and girl lines.

Ideas from Inside Joleen's Classroom

♦ Children's safety is one compelling argument for providing antihomophobia education.

♦ Breaking the silence about LGBT and issues of difference, and responding to students who discriminate, can inspire confidence in both teachers and students to react to other acts of injustice that arise in school life.

♦ An inclusive atmosphere is best realized when the efforts of the entire school are harnessed to achieve this goal.

CHAPTER 4

A White Teacher's Quest to Become a Culturally Responsive Teacher: Mary Williams

Mary Williams grew up in white suburbia—a very different background from that of the African American and Latino fourth graders she teaches in a low-income community of New York City's East Harlem. As a new teacher she was eager to learn about her students, to understand them, and to provide them with meaningful experiences. Mary understood that children learn best in contexts that are interesting, relevant, and purposeful. Therefore she searched for ways to offer her students materials and experiences that would resonate with their lives, interest and engage them, and help them see themselves in their learning. In this way she hoped to ensure that they would develop an ongoing love of learning while also meeting the school system's expectations.

To begin her work on these goals, Mary read about culturally responsive teaching. From her study she learned of the need for teachers to present the world to children through a variety of perspectives and to provide students with positive images of many different cultures, especially those represented by the children in their classrooms.[10] She wanted to do more than observe the token holiday, week, or month that the mainstream culture offered in acknowledgment of an ethnic or racial group.[11] She also came to realize that her experience as a member of the white majority shaped her thinking in ways she had not formerly been aware of and she became sensitized to how important it was for her to learn to view the world through others' eyes. With the population of children in the public school system of the United States becoming increasingly diverse, she understood that *all* teachers (the majority of whom are white) need to keep this awareness at the forefront of their consciousness. To help herself do this, Mary decided to devote the school year to observation and reflection about cultural diversity and how she could teach in ways that would honor it.

CHALLENGES IN A REAL-LIFE CLASSROOM

Unprepared for the Unexpected

One of the challenges that Mary faced in her efforts to be a culturally responsive teacher revolved around how to facilitate discussions of socially relevant ideas and events. Although she felt pretty comfortable introducing multicultural materials into the curriculum, she was less confident about how to get beyond superficial beginnings. The other issue she struggled with (and this one really surprised her) was how to react sensitively to children's perspectives on real-life issues and events. Sometimes children's comments were quite jarring to her middle-class, liberal sensitivities. For example, at the very beginning of the school year, Mary launched a study in her classroom about heroes. She read the children a book about courage by a renowned children's author; it looked at the various ways in which kids, the occasional grown-up, and even one very endearing dog displayed bravery.[12] The message the book conveyed was that there are many different kinds of courage. As she facilitated a class discussion about the book, the events of September 11, 2001, and the demise of the World Trade Center's twin towers came up. Because her students were young when 9/11 occurred, Mary had assumed that they knew nothing about it. She soon realized, however, that several of them had learned about it through their parents and had incorporated their parents' perspectives on the event. "My mom said the devil came out and decided to hit the towers," one child offered in the discussion. Mary was at a loss as to how to respond: "I didn't want to get into the politics of 9/11, discussions of the war, or the religious beliefs of my students. I am still uncertain of where the place of the teacher is within those areas."

Mary also was uncertain about what to do when her students shared information that highlighted differences in how they were being raised—issues of how their family members disciplined and communicated with them. For example, when teaching the book *Fourth Grade Rats*,[13] a story about peer pressure, rebellion, and the importance of being oneself, her goal was to help the students make connections between the book and their own lives. She asked her students what would happen if they said "no" to their parents. Mary's intention in raising this question was to help her students understand the action of the main character in the story, who was rebellious to his mother. One spoke up to say that her mother would "pop me in the face" if she said "no" to her. She then shared stories of how she was disciplined at home, describing physical punishments that were outside the realm of Mary's view of acceptability. While Mary realized that the differences between her perspective on discipline and that of this child's family were influenced by their respective cultural backgrounds, she nevertheless felt quite uncomfortable and unsure of how to react.

Differences like these frequently arose. While working on writing exercises, stressful home experiences of some children were revealed, leaving Mary unsure about how to respond. For instance, when students were crafting personal narratives, some included details of their lives, such as gunshots in the street, "crazy drunken neighbors," and the dangers of "the projects" in which they lived.

As Mary reflected on her reaction to these experiences that were so far removed from her own, she came to realize how little she had really understood, when she first began teaching, about the realities of her students' lives. She wondered if educator preparation for white middle-class teachers might be more effective if it included more experiences in urban settings and more discussion about the challenges of these contexts. "Coming from a completely different culture . . . put me at a disadvantage of not knowing what to expect to hear about their lives." If she had had a stronger idea of what to expect, Mary reasoned, she might have been more skillful and sensitive about framing questions and reacting to the information students shared.

Fitting It In

Another challenge Mary confronted was how to fit culturally relevant and responsive teaching into the school's prescribed curriculum. As a new teacher, Mary first struggled to "just get by," trying to make sure that she taught what the school defined as "essential." Consumed with her efforts to understand the strict curriculum guidelines for literacy and mathematics that she was required to follow, she had little energy left over for learning how to make her teaching culturally relevant. She worried too that the administration would not be happy if she digressed from the prescribed curriculum.

Making It Work

Mary was determined to find a way to meet the school system's expectations without abandoning the practices and principles of responsive teaching that she had learned would enhance her students' learning. She did this by infusing culturally relevant materials into her read-aloud choices, by adapting math problems to reflect the realities of children's lives, by encouraging students to share their ideas and life experiences, and by creating a sense of community in the classroom.

Adapting the Curriculum   Determined to adapt the rigidly prescribed curriculum to work in a more culturally relevant way, Mary kept a journal of reflections about her teaching to play with ideas of how to meet the demands of the administration as well as her own and her students' needs. For example, in a required mathematics lesson about graphing, in which the students were asked to demonstrate their knowledge of pictographs by creating a graph, she changed the text's original assignment of creating a class graph of students' favorite foods to creating a class graph of "Where are you all originally from?" After inviting the children to talk in small groups about their families' places of origin, they each shared a bit about their home countries, which included New York, Puerto Rico, the Dominican Republic, and Haiti. In the midst of the animated discussions, which included lots of questions about their cultures and the places where they were born, Mary taught the children how to make tally charts and other pictographs of the data. She was pleased to have found a way to create opportunities for meaningful conversations while still meeting the aim of the required lesson.

Infusing culturally relevant read-aloud books into the literacy curriculum was an idea Mary gleaned from reading the work of Gloria Ladson-Billings, a leading educator of culturally responsive teaching.[14] Ladson-Billings's work led Mary to consciously select texts for the class to read that had characters from diverse backgrounds. She chose *The Stories Julian Tells*, a book based in the African American experience.[15] From the very first chapter, Mary noticed that her students found ways to connect the book with their lives: "We had a long conversation about important customs in our families' lives just like Julian had had with his family when they made pudding together. I shared how my family makes sauce every summer together on the anniversary of my father's death. The students then shared traditions they have with their families—like making tacos, beans and rice, and cake together." From this experience Mary realized that "the books I know from my childhood . . . connected with me because it was *me* I was reading about." From then on she carefully selected texts for her students that had characters and experiences with which they could relate. She noticed this made them more motivated to read.

Opportunities for Sharing   The more opportunities Mary provided for her students to share their life experiences in the classroom, the more engaged they became in their learning. She noticed her students asking each other more thoughtful questions and becoming increasingly attentive in their class discussions. Little by little she was figuring out ways to "see students' cultural capital as an asset and not a detriment to their school success."[16] A math lesson on geometry offers a great example of this. As an introduction to geometric shapes, Mary read to the class the book *Sam Johnson and the Blue Ribbon Quilt*, a book about a man who starts an all-male quilting club.[17] Her intention in presenting this book was to motivate the students to create a paper quilt using the different shapes they were learning about. A discussion ensued, however, about male and female roles. Although many of the children reacted in a stereotypical way to the portrayal of men involved in quilting, one of the children in the class shared information about his family that offered a different perspective for the children to entertain. Joseph, a generally timid and quiet child, blurted out, "Quilting is very important in my family." Although taken a bit by surprise, Mary stopped the official lesson on geometry and asked Joseph to share more. Curious, the students asked many questions, which Joseph was only too pleased to answer. This little detour served not only to validate Joseph, his family, and their culture and traditions, it also sparked the children's interest in the project Mary had planned for them to do. Although the lesson had changed, the math aim was accomplished.

BUILDING COMMUNITY

As a result of the time Mary invested in creating a space for the children to share their ideas, backgrounds, and cultures, a sense of community developed in the classroom. Her modeling of how to be a good listener and her assistance to children as they got to know each other helped to establish trusting relationships. As the school year progressed, the benefits of her efforts were increasingly evident. For instance, at the conclusion of a writing study, the class celebrated by holding a "publishing party," during which the children shared stories of their lives with each other and invited guests. Mary was pleased to note that everyone in the class felt comfortable reading their original work to the others. She was especially pleased to observe Daniel, an English language learner who spoke with a stutter and was usually nervous about speaking in public, enthusiastically sharing what he had written. The speech coach who had worked with Daniel was amazed. After witnessing him reading, she told Mary that she had never before seen Daniel so at ease. No doubt the trusting atmosphere developed in the classroom helped Daniel feel secure enough to take the risks necessary to so freely share information about himself.

Another aspect of building community in the classroom is making connections with students' lives *outside* the classroom.[18] Mary made efforts to do this by attending neighborhood events and cultural performances that her students were participating in. In such informal contexts she was able to get to know and understand them and their families in broader ways. Her efforts were not only appreciated but further enhanced the relationship building that is so critical for supporting children's learning.

OBSERVING, DOCUMENTING, AND REFLECTING TO SUPPORT CULTURALLY RESPONSIVE TEACHING

Looking back on the experiences she has had learning about and trying to become a responsive teacher to the diverse groups of children in her urban classroom, Mary credits much of her accomplishment to the research skills she relied on during the investigation recounted here. Her project got her in the habit of observing and documenting her students at work in the classroom. And then each day after school she reflected on the information she had collected during the day. "Those twenty minutes spent writing my reflections in my journal is where so many questions were answered and where my teaching practices and ability to reach students grew. Now I still take the time to reflect; it is a necessary part of my growing as a teacher and a learner."

Since Mary began her efforts to become a more culturally responsive teacher, she has incorporated research into her practice, using it to shape and guide her curriculum. Now in her third year of teaching, she has developed a comprehensive data collection system that literally drives her instruction. She uses what she learns from the evidence she collects to structure small instructional groups as well as to inform her one-on-one conferencing with students. Working in this way has helped her, she believes, to teach more effectively so that her students succeed.

Being culturally responsive and relevant continues to be a challenge for Mary. As a result of her investigation of this issue, however, she regularly asks herself, "What would make this learning matter?" to guide her in meeting her students' needs.

Ideas from Inside Mary's Classroom

♦ It can be challenging to teach children from cultural backgrounds that are different from one's own. Careful observation and listening, along with reflection and a critical stance on one's assumptions, are all useful tools in being culturally responsive.

♦ Investing time in activities to help children get to know each other has the potential to build a strong classroom community and can foster the students' abilities to establish trusting relationships.

♦ Taking the time to learn about students' lives enables teachers to understand them better as well as to use their cultures and experiences as resources for learning.

♦ Carefully selecting texts that feature characters and experiences the students can relate to can captivate and motivate children to read and learn.

Inside School/Family Partnerships

In this section we feature the work of five educators who have built school/family partnerships that bridge differences across cultures, languages, and socioeconomic backgrounds. While each one of their stories is unique, together they reveal important insights about how to effectively work with families from diverse backgrounds. The stories help us understand

- how important it is for teachers and school administrators to reach out across languages and cultures to develop effective ways to communicate with and involve families in the learning life of schools;

- how much family members know about their children that can be a valuable asset to the teaching/learning process;

- how the knowledge, skills, and strengths of each family can be used to support their children's learning;

- how deeply parents and caregivers, no matter their circumstance, care about their children and their children's education.

CHAPTER 5

Bridging the Language Gap: Evelyn Chang

Evelyn Chang is a Chinese American who grew up speaking Chinese at home and did not learn English until she entered school. Her parents spoke what she described as "broken English" and they often relied on her to clarify what her teachers said. Her own memories of the pressure and stress of being a child translator for her parents caused her, when she became a third-grade teacher in a predominantly Spanish-speaking community in New York City's East Harlem, to purposely not use children to translate conversations with parents and to rely instead on other adults. However, she was dissatisfied with the quality of the information she was getting from the adult translators, so she decided to investigate how to "break the language barrier" with the Spanish-speaking family members of her students.

EVELYN'S INQUIRY

Evelyn had empathy for many of her students whose families were new immigrants to the United States with very little knowledge of English, because her own parents had been in a similar position many years ago. However, there were some aspects of her students' parents' situations that were quite different from her own. Unlike the parents of the children in her class, Evelyn's own parents were older and highly educated. Evelyn explained that in the suburban New Jersey community in which she grew up, most parents were involved in the school, and although "the education culture here [in the United States] wasn't necessarily familiar to them, they [Evelyn's parents] saw everybody else's parents being involved, and they just went along with it." Evelyn compared this to the norms in the last two schools in which she worked: "Here, even if you've moved from somewhere else into the neighborhood, you see the other parents not involved, so there is little initiative to go out and do it on your own. . . ."

Examining the Translation Process

Because she wanted to improve communication with the non-English-speaking families in her class, Evelyn set out to examine her parent conferences and the role of translations during these events. In the hopes that this investigation would make her relationships with families more effective, Evelyn selected three parents to study in depth. Each was a non-English-speaker and each had a different level of involvement in Evelyn's class. She began by interviewing each parent with a translator. Then she had another translator help her to translate the audiotapes of the conversations. The following excerpt from one of the conversations reveals some surprising things that Evelyn learned from her investigation:

Evelyn: So what does Austin like to do at home?

Translator: What does Austin enjoy doing at home? Does he like to play sports, read, watch TV?

Parent: Austin likes to watch a lot of TV. He likes the . . . Discover show . . . He likes science. (Pause.) He doesn't like to read. I have to make him. I take away TV if he doesn't read.

Translator: It's great that he likes science. Maybe you should get some science books, take him to the library. You know, use something he's interested in.

Parent: His babysitter takes him to the library. I don't have the time because I work. But he takes out comics. But he doesn't read them. I think he just looks at the pictures. He likes to draw too.

Translator (interrupts): You know Austin is reading at a very low grade level; he's very behind. You really need to make sure he is reading every night.

Evelyn: What did she say?

Translator: She said that Austin doesn't like to read at home. She's frustrated with him because she can't get him to read.

Discoveries

After reading this translated transcript, Evelyn was shocked to learn that she had been missing out on valuable information that took place in the interchanges between the parent and the translator. For example, the translator totally left out the information that Austin's babysitter took him to the library and that he liked comics—information that might have been able to help her pique Austin's interest in literacy. She also realized that she was not getting a "true" answer to her questions because the translator had given Austin's mother additional prompts to Evelyn's questions that significantly changed the nature of the responses. From examining just this one interview, Evelyn learned that the translator had six outside conversations (sometimes quite lengthy) and had inserted her own advice or opinion nine times. Writing in her journal after this conference, Evelyn reflected: "I can't believe how much goes on that I'm unaware of! From Austin's mother getting defensive, to the translator giving her own advice . . . I may as well have not been there at all. I don't know what to make of this, or where to go from here."

Trying Out Translation Strategies

Seeking to remedy these problems, Evelyn subsequently experimented with strategies to make translations of her communications with non-English-speaking parents work more effectively and to strengthen her efforts to engage them more in the life of the classroom. She explored assisting in the translation process by emphasizing her emotions when speaking to the parent through the translator. For instance, when the translator told one parent the good news that her daughter always brings in her homework, Evelyn made sure to smile directly at the mother to help convey the message. In addition, Evelyn began to confer with the translator before the parent/teacher conferences to explicitly make clear the need for accuracy in the translations and to caution the translator not to hold extraneous conversations.

After initiating these changes, Evelyn noticed improvement when she read the translated audiotapes of subsequent conferences. Not only did she find that the translator inserted her own opinions far less, but she identified far fewer instances of inaccurate translator accounts of exchanges that took place between her and a caregiver. A preconference conversation with her translator, Evelyn learned, made for a much more productive conference.

Reaching Out to Families

In the course of her investigation Evelyn also developed new ways to reach out to families. One was to provide what Evelyn called "quick-fix translator messages" at dismissal or drop-off time. These were simple communications about events in her classroom that were conveyed by Spanish-speaking volunteers whom Evelyn had identified and trained. As a result of employing these volunteers to share information, Evelyn began to notice that parents relied less on their own children to translate for them. Often she found them eagerly waiting for the volunteer so that they could find out the latest classroom news.

Capitalizing on the parents' newfound comfort level at the school, Evelyn invited them to join in classroom events and to observe in the classroom. For instance, she invited them to a publishing party in her classroom where the bilingual parents translated information and the Spanish-speaking children excitedly translated their own stories after reading them in English. One Spanish-speaking parent reflected later to Evelyn that her favorite part of the day was seeing her daughter read in English.

Evelyn's experiences of being a child of immigrant parents who struggled with the English language probably made her more sensitive than most teachers to the non-English-speaking families of her students. However, her careful work of studying her conversations with them and of documenting how she found ways to include them in classroom life heightened her sensitivity even more and improved her relationships with them. During and after her study of this issue, she noticed a significant rise in attendance of non-English-speaking families at classroom events.

SHARING HER LEARNING

When Evelyn shared the findings of her study with other urban teachers, many of whom worked in similar communities, her colleagues shared that they too had difficulty attracting non-English-speaking parents to their school events. Admitting that, before hearing about Evelyn's study, they had simply assumed that the parents in their classes weren't interested in being involved, they acknowledged that they were now rethinking these assumptions. Evelyn's study thus not only challenged her own thinking about how she could reach out to families who spoke languages other than English, it also sparked dialogue with other teachers that led them to be more sensitive to others' perspectives and to respond to the families of the children in their classes in a way that enhanced family involvement.

PUTTING NEW UNDERSTANDING INTO PRACTICE

Three years after conducting her study, as she reflected on how it had helped her to strengthen and increase parent involvement in her classroom, Evelyn reported that her new understanding had resulted in her current assistant principal jokingly calling her "high maintenance and crazy" for all the special requests and events she now designs on behalf of her students' families. She communicates with most of them through e-mail, using a Google tool to translate the messages she sends and receives. She still confers with translators prior to parent/teacher conferences, and she is now studying Spanish so that she can better communicate directly with more families. Two to three parents a week volunteer in her class. Having recently moved to a new school setting (which is also in a predominantly Spanish-speaking neighborhood), she continues to hold publishing parties and other family events in her classroom, all of which are well attended. Reflecting on all of these changes, Evelyn said,

> I'm a better teacher now than I ever thought I would be. I remember my first two years being, like, "Man, are these kids going to learn anything?" And now I honestly complete each year pretty satisfied about where they are when they leave me. . . . I learned that, you know, that old saying [is true]: If you don't ask you won't get. And I feel like if you ask the parents to [get] involved, and you continuously reach out to them, they eventually do.

Evelyn continues to conduct research about her teaching, now as part of a study group in her school. Meeting every other Friday, the group, which is facilitated by reading coaches in her school, first focused on differentiated instruction. Evelyn said, "It was a like a book club where we tested out different strategies to see how they would or wouldn't work in our classrooms. . . . Things like that, when other people are involved, make teaching seem easier and more fun." Her experience with her colleagues is testimony to the notion of Oakes, Franke, Quartz, and Rogers[1] that powerful teacher learning happens when there is a joint engagement to develop mutually valued work.

As Evelyn has continued to learn about working with families, she has realized how her attitudes and ideas have changed and how much she has grown since she began investigating how to deal with families in her classroom who don't speak English. For example, instead of thinking of families as being "resistant," as she did only a short time ago, she now realizes that a better characterization of their behavior is "hesitant." Evelyn has come to understand that families often don't get involved simply because they don't feel welcomed in school. "If parents feel welcomed, then they will come in to discuss what you want to discuss. They have to feel welcomed all year long."

Ideas from Inside Evelyn's Classroom

♦ Try to get translators to assist in communicating with families whose language you do not know.

♦ Hold a preconference conversation with the translator to pave the way for a productive conference.

♦ Emphasize facial expressions when speaking to the translator in front of parents to assist in the translation process.

♦ Ask bilingual parents to volunteer to deliver "quick-fix translator messages" at dismissal or drop-off time.

♦ Use translating tools, even though they're imperfect, to make it possible to e-mail non-English-speaking parents.

♦ Ask bilingual parents or children to translate stories at publishing parties and other classroom events in order to make visiting the classroom more inviting to non-English-speaking parents.

CHAPTER 6

Addressing the Unspoken: Joan O'Brien

Even after twenty-five years of experience working as a preschool teacher, with five years of those in a Head Start program in East Harlem, Joan felt she needed to learn more about how she could help teachers, children, and their families ease the transition from home to early schooling. Describing how time after time she witnessed children crying, sometimes uncontrollably, when their parents left them in the classroom, she noted that "it is often disturbing to see some children cry in real distress. . . ." Determined to figure out how to make transitions between home and school more comfortable, she decided to investigate children's perspectives about transitioning to school in order to better understand separation anxiety.

JOAN'S BACKGROUND

Joan's own childhood experiences, while different from those of the children whom she taught, informed her thinking about what makes for a comfortable transition to child care. Unlike her urban students who were primarily of Dominican, Mexican, and African American descent, Joan grew up in rural Guyana. She did not remember having problems separating as a young child and reasoned that this might have been because at that time in Guyana the preschools were in people's homes and she went to school just a couple of streets from her house. Joan recollected that "the teacher was a motherly person . . . . Her kitchen was right there, you used to be smelling her food cooking."

There were additional aspects of Joan's background that she suspected contributed to her easy transition and comfortable adjustment to school when she was a child. Among these were that she came from a big family—she was one of ten children. Reflecting on how this affected her, she said, "I was just anxious to go to school because you would always see the bigger ones go to school." Joan also attributed her smooth transition to school to the fact that she lived in a "close-knit" community where "if you did anything wrong, anybody in the community could have spoken to you or rebuked you." Growing up in such a close, caring community informed Joan's thinking as she embarked on her investigation of separation anxiety. Her goal was to help children in their most vulnerable years make a smooth transition to school and create an environment in which they felt cared for and safe.

EXPLORING THE PERSPECTIVES OF THE CHILDREN

To gain insight to how to do this, Joan studied six children and their families. She observed the children while they were at school, interviewed their parents, and held discussions with three other teachers in her school about what strategies they found to be successful in promoting smooth home/school transitions. She also created questions for the parents to ask their children at home, which they then reported back to her. In her new role as teacher-researcher, Joan came to see her very familiar classroom with "new eyes." She began to see things that she had not noticed before, like the children who seemed okay because they did not cry when their parents left but whose difficulties were expressed in more subtle ways. Although they were quiet and unobtrusive, these children had "glazed expressions," a symptom of distress she had read about in the educational literature. Myisha was one of these quietly distressed children. In the past, Joan admitted, she might not have been concerned about Myisha's expressionless stance. But through her investigation she learned that, like the crying child, this reaction to separating from caregivers needed to be handled with care and sensitivity. Sure enough, when Joan probed Myisha about her feelings one day as Myisha sat with her doll next to Joan in a quiet manner that could have been mistaken for everything being okay, Myisha suddenly let out a wail of, "I want my mommy." Joan's study was making her more aware of the need to look beneath the surface of children's behaviors in order to learn about their true feelings.

Joan continued her quest to better understand her children's and their families' perspectives by examining the responses to the interviews she had asked parents to hold with their children at the end of the school day. From these she learned how the children felt about school and what they enjoyed about their days. The question that informed Joan the most about the children and their needs was, "What do you want to do when you get to school tomorrow?" The children's responses helped her to get a sense of their preferences and their interests, which Joan then used to plan her curriculum. Realizing how important it is for the learning environment to build on children's interests and strengths, Joan eventually made this question a regular part of the school day, asking the children in their late afternoon meeting to choose the activity they wanted to pursue during the upcoming day's Choice Time. "I found that this strategy worked well in helping the children anticipate and look forward to attending school the following day."

Motivated by the educational literature she read as a background for her study, Joan began to seek out children's perspectives and expectations about other matters so that she could better understand the context of their lives. As she talked and listened to them more and more carefully, she learned about the layers of concerns that many brought into the classroom.

HIDDEN STRESSORS

Sarah was an example of a child who came to school weighed down with family-related concerns. One of the children who cried the most at the beginning of the school year, Sarah was not only sad about leaving her mother, but she was also worried *about* her. Joan's conversations with Sarah revealed that Sarah and her mother had just moved to a shelter and that Sarah was apprehensive about her mother's well-being while she was away at school. Becoming aware of the enormous burden that this little person was carrying around gave a broader perspective to Sarah's inconsolable crying. Once this was clear to Joan, she talked to Sarah about her fears and opened up a dialogue with Sarah's mother. Together Joan and Sarah's mother were able to reassure the child and calm her fears. This experience made Joan keenly aware that even though learning to separate from family is a natural part of life for all children, the stresses of life for those who are poor can profoundly affect a child's schooling experiences and can confound this already difficult time.

After successfully navigating Sarah's adjustment to school, Joan was saddened that Sarah did not return in the fall. "Just as I was getting close to her and she was getting close to me," Joan explained, "Sarah suddenly disappeared. I often think about her and wonder what she is doing. . . ." This was a poignant reminder that having a child suddenly and mysteriously leave school, after investing oneself in the relationship, is a loss that is not uncommon for those who teach in low-income communities.

STRATEGIES FOR EASING
THE HOME/SCHOOL TRANSITION

In the course of her study, Joan developed several strategies to help her students ease the transition between home and school. Enlisting the support of the families and using them as the valuable resource she was coming to understand them to be, she worked to learn as much as she could from parents about their children in order to make all of them feel more comfortable. For example, she tried using the parents' "pet names" for their children and asked the parents to bring in special toys or blankets and photos from home to help the children bridge home and school. Additionally, because she learned that the cultural traditions of many of her children's parents discouraged families from getting involved with the school and/or that many parents were reluctant to interact because of their own negative childhood educational experiences, Joan spent quite a bit of time reaching out to parents, explaining the curriculum, and trying to help them understand how what she was doing in the classroom supported the ways that children learn. She shared with them at length about what they could expect their children to experience during the school year and encouraged them to engage in educational activities at home, offering ideas about materials and books that they could easily obtain. Working with the families in these ways, Joan was able to create a more welcoming and accepting learning environment.

LESSONS LEARNED

Joan's research project stays with her in her current work with children and families. Two important new understandings stand out: First, she has transformed her image of the role of a teacher from that of an authority figure to a partner with parents in the care of their children. Joan realized as a result of her study that "I shouldn't be telling parents about their children, but sharing *with* parents. The thing is that parents can be sensitive, so instead of saying 'Your child is so-so-so,' you could instead say, 'Let me share something with you.' So that whatever you are saying belongs to both of us. I'm sharing it with you and then asking you what do you think?" Additionally, Joan has become more sensitized to the perspectives of her students and their families. As a result, she has become more respectful of them. "Parents know their children better than the teachers do. We can learn a lot from parents about their children. I realize now that we need to respect parents—all parents. They only want the best for their children."

Ideas from Inside Joan's Classroom

♦ Some children may show distress in subtle ways; therefore, careful observation of all children's behaviors is necessary in order to understand and react to how they are feeling.

♦ Even though learning to separate from family is a natural part of life for all children, the stresses of life for those who are poor can profoundly affect a child's schooling experiences and can confound this already difficult time.

♦ Asking anxious children to express their choices of activities for the next day at school can help to get a sense of the children's preferences and provide information to use in planning the curriculum.

♦ Regularly communicating with parents about what their children are learning in school and why it's important can help parents expand on school experiences at home.

♦ Partnering with parents in the care of their children, rather than taking on the role of the sole authority, results in better understanding and support that can help the entire family.

CHAPTER 7

Incorporating Families' Funds of Knowledge into the Classroom: Kanene Holder

Kanene Holder, a science cluster teacher at a charter school in East Harlem, has long had an interest in her students' home cultures. Fascinated with the idea that "what you think a group of people are might not necessarily be who they are," Kanene traces the origins of this belief to the assumptions made about her when she was young. Growing up in a Caribbean neighborhood in Flatbush, Brooklyn, with a mother originally from Jamaica and a father from Trinidad, Kanene for most of her childhood went to schools serving children from predominantly Caribbean backgrounds. However, in high school she traveled nearly an hour and a half to Sheepshead Bay, a neighborhood in the outer reaches of Brooklyn, where she attended a school with a mostly white population. Here she experienced racial and cultural prejudice. Kanene explains:

> The children I was in school with assumed that because I'm black that I was African American. And it's like, no, I'm Caribbean and it's

a totally different thing. [T]he foods we eat are different, the way we talk is different, the proverbs we use are different, it's a totally different culture. You might not see that because as far as you're concerned I'm the same color as this next person, so what's the difference? But to me it was a huge difference.

Kanene said that the kids called her "'Buckwheat,' . . . made fun of my hair, and would say that I ate watermelon and fried chicken all the time." It wasn't until she attended Howard University and went to school with a large population of American black students that she realized that these behaviors were not just cruel, but in fact racist. And she came also to recognize how damaging these experiences had been to her own educational and personal development. So when she became an educator, she vowed never to forget how they impacted her and she committed herself to being sensitive and responsive to her students and their cultures. She was determined to find out "Who are these people? Who are these children that I'm teaching, who are these parents? I can't assume I know who they are. I have to go about a process of finding out who they are."

LEARNING ABOUT FAMILIES' FUNDS OF KNOWLEDGE

While in graduate school to obtain her teacher certification, Kanene learned of a theory called "funds of knowledge" that resonated with her desires to better understand her students.[2] "Funds of knowledge" is a framework for understanding teaching that draws attention to the important role that family and community knowledge play in supporting children's learning. It posits that each family and community has knowledge found in their daily experiences—such as their work, their ceremonies or rituals, the way they manage finances or prepare food—that is often overlooked and not valued by mainstream culture. Educators informed by the theory of "funds of knowledge" use an anthropological approach to learning about their students' environments, visiting their students' homes, and conducting interviews of their students' families and other key community members. They then draw on what they have learned to develop curricula relevant to their students' experiences and understanding, partnering with their students' families and community and using them as resources for the children's learning. The idea behind this approach is that children come to school not as blank slates but actually knowing a great deal that has been acquired from the model of their community's adults. Teachers who work together with their students' families and caregivers, who invite the families to educate them about what the children come to school knowing, and who include the wisdom of the community in their classrooms without categorizing, labeling, or making a static definition of any group of people, then use this understanding to ensure more effective teaching.

In an effort to improve her teaching, Kanene decided to investigate the funds of knowledge of her students and their families. She began by visiting with three parents: Cory and Monica, whom she had met at a school barbeque, and Raquel, the chairperson of the school's parent board.

UNFORESEEN CHALLENGES

Originally, Kanene's plan for her "funds of knowledge" investigation had been to visit with all three of the parents at home, at school, and during community excursions. Her expectations had been that through her visits she would learn about the richness of their lives—"visually, musically, linguistically, artistically, and in many other ways." Instead she encountered all sorts of difficulties that she had not anticipated. For example, each one of the parents had a hard time making time to talk with her, often canceling at the last minute or missing the appointment altogether. This was often because the circumstances of their lives were more complicated than Kanene had ever imagined them to be. For example, Kanene learned that Cory was in and out of the hospital suffering from several serious medical

conditions; that Raquel, a working single mother, juggled multiple responsibilities that included caring for her own mom as well as her nephew; and
that Monica, who was unemployed and living in a shelter, was not reachable
by phone because Monica did not pay the bill and, as a result, it had been
disconnected. None of this was what Kanene had expected when she set
out to learn about her students' families. Only through her efforts to reach
out did she gain an understanding of the numerous obstacles and stressors
in their lives.

UNEXPECTED LESSONS

But Kanene's efforts to become more knowledgeable about her students'
families helped her to understand that their lives were more than just their
problems. She also came to see that each and every parent held a deep,
abiding love for their child that transcended any of the challenges that they
faced. Kanene learned, for example, that despite the fact that Cory was
seriously ill, she kept track of every event in her daughter's school life, re-
ferring regularly to school documents that she kept and displayed on the
refrigerator in the kitchen of her home. Even in hospital-bed conversations
with Kanene, Cory did not dwell on her battles with illness but instead
spoke frequently of her hopes and dreams to provide a safe and nurturing
environment for her daughter and of her desire to be a positive model for
her daughter of how to focus on the future and "work through the pain."

From her developing relationship with Cory, Kanene gained a newfound
respect for the parents with whom she worked. What she learned provided
her with a counternarrative to our culture's prevailing stereotypes about
the urban poor. She realized that despite the obstacles that they face, be it a
lack of education or financial security, parents love and have big dreams for
their children. They "want to see their children succeed and *do* care about
their future."

Inspired particularly by Cory's dreams and by how hard Cory was working to pull her life together, Kanene committed herself to doing her personal best in her teaching. Reflecting on what she learned from Cory, Kanene said:

> Seeing [Cory] be as committed to being a parent as she was despite her ailments taught me a lesson about love and selflessness. At times I can become frustrated because something didn't go as I had planned in the classroom, but knowing about [Cory's] life and the lives of others allows me to see myself in a position of power and as an agent of change no matter how difficult the situation may seem. I have learned to enjoy the art of teaching and *listening*. Because she was such a good model of compassion, I had no choice but to be open and listen.

From conducting her study, Kanene came to realize that "we teachers sometimes have limiting assumptions about parents." She resolved to make every effort in the future to move beyond such limited assumptions and try to more fully understand the lives and experiences of her students and their families.

INTEGRATING NEW UNDERSTANDING INTO THE CLASSROOM

As time has gone by, Kanene has woven into her teaching and her curriculum her growing understanding of her students, their parents, and their community. Recently she launched a study with her students on the gentrification and rezoning of her school's neighborhood. Using pictures, newspaper articles, and maps of the area, she held discussions and debates with the class about issues and challenges facing the community. She also took the class on a tour of the neighborhood, during which they noticed many closed stores. This prompted discussion of the struggling economy and the importance of supporting local businesses, especially the family-owned stores in the area.

In addition to incorporating the children's interests and their knowledge of the community into the work of her classroom, Kanene also has led her students in investigations of the different cultures they represent. They have explored a nearby Native American community and begun a study of Asian cultures, launched after a visit to a local Japanese restaurant.

From Kanene's perspective, her research about her students' families was one of the most significant experiences she has had as a teacher. It made her more aware that the homes of her urban students are important places for learning and that parents are their children's most important educators. Most powerfully, it also made her realize the depth of the love parents have for their children and what a privilege and honor it is for teachers to have parents entrust children to their care. Kanene hopes that being featured in this book will extend this awareness to the wider teaching community: "I hope my study will spark curiosity in educators to discover the wealth of knowledge within their school's community and elevate the role of the parent from just a guardian and disciplinarian to being an educator."

Ideas from Inside Kanene's Classroom

♦ In the same way that teachers need to seek understanding of their students through multiple venues, teachers also need to learn about parents with an equally open mind.

♦ Use your students' families and the community as resources for your students' learning.

♦ Learn about the "richness of their lives" of one or two families in your classroom in an in-depth way.

♦ Draw on what you have learned about families in your classroom to develop curricula relevant to your students' experiences and understanding.

CHAPTER 8

Bridging Differences: Rory Scott

Rory Scott, just prior to the time of this writing, was the director of the Harbor Morningside Children's Center, an early-childhood center in central Harlem that had been recognized nationally for its outstanding practice. Recently closed due to citywide budget cuts, the center was part of a larger agency that provides a range of social services to low-income children and families in the community. Although the center is no longer operating and Rory has moved on to another position, his story is recounted here to share some of the important learning that he gained through his study and his work.

Born, raised, and educated in Harlem, Rory continues to live there with his family and has deep ties to the community. He began volunteering in after-school programs as a teenager, returning to this work after a number of intervening years as a musician. In the course of his teaching he distinguished himself as an educator to such a degree that he was recruited to become the Harbor Morningside Center's director. After accepting that position he demonstrated his commitment to education and service not only through his leadership but also by volunteering his skills in a variety of other ways. He is an active member of the church he attended when he was a child, leading so many of the church-related musical groups that some mistake him for the congregation's music director. Additionally, he mentors a number of young people in the neighborhood, including a young woman from Senegal who was employed at his center. She benefited so much from their relationship that her family asked Rory to become her godfather and invited him to visit them in Africa. While honored by this recognition, Rory explained his contributions in this way: "For most of my life I have made it my own personal mission to help to improve the lives of the people of Harlem through education and spiritual development, starting with the seed—the children."

CONTEXT

Although Harlem is known as an African American community, the neighborhood surrounding Rory's former center has a large population of African immigrants, part of a sizable influx that has taken place within the last two decades in the United States in general and, more specifically, in New York City. These newcomers to the United States have settled in West Harlem, an area heavily populated by people who, for the most part, share their ancestry. Children from these families made up a significant portion of those who attended the center. And with them, Rory felt a special connection:

I have always felt a special connection with the continent of Africa. Even though I didn't begin to learn true black history until I was a teenager, my early exposure to Africa, through magazines and music, took me there in a special way quite often. No one in my family could trace our lineage back any further than Eastville, Virginia, but my grandmother's *National Geographic* magazines, coupled with my mother's Miriam Makeba albums, apparently forged a bond so strong in a young boy's heart that it still exists today. I grew up loving the music, the land, and the people.

It wasn't until I started in the position of director at Harbor Morningside Children's Center that I had the opportunity to deal with African immigrants on a daily basis. I was very excited when I found out we had a couple of African immigrant families as clients at the center. I quickly developed a close relationship with them. It was then that I began to hear the stories of their struggles to get their children into day care and the obstacles they faced. They were frequently ignored, turned away, or put on endless waiting lists, never to be called. I decided to make sure things like that would never happen at Harbor Morningside.

To fulfill this promise, Rory began by learning more about his immigrant neighbors and what he could do to address their needs. Through readings about immigration, his own observations, interviews, and surveys with parents, teachers, and other staff, as well as through his reflections about his work, Rory deepened his insights into the challenges African immigrants encounter as they interact with and attempt to navigate their children's educational institutions. This helped him to develop practices that were supportive of them and their needs.

One of the first things Rory learned was that there is a great deal of diversity within the African families in the Harlem community. The majority of them are from the Ivory Coast. The rest are from Senegal, Mali, Ghana, Sierra Leone, Gambia, and Nigeria. All of these groupings of people—all from West Africa—were represented in the population at Harbor Morningside. The rest of the center's population came from Puerto Rico, the Dominican Republic, Belize, and, of course, the continental United States.

THE CHALLENGES: AN OVERVIEW

African immigrants, Rory learned, face many challenges and problems in their new land. As he explains, "Like most other immigrants settling on American shores, African immigrants seek to take part in the American dream of freedom and prosperity. What they have found upon their arrival, however, are cultural barriers that prevent them from being easily assimilated into our society."

Language Barriers

One of the main barriers for African immigrants, Rory discovered, is language. While West Africans often speak French in addition to several local home languages, more often than not they do not speak English. As a result, they have tremendous communication challenges that make it difficult for them to access needed services. Unfortunately, little help is available from the extensive translation services that New York City provides for the speakers of the 180 or so different languages in the schools. Surprisingly, French is not one of the languages into which information is translated. As Rory explains:

> Information from the local and city level is distributed in English and Spanish and, in some cases, Chinese, but never in French or in any of the African dialects. There are translation services for Spanish-speaking parents but, again, none for French-speaking parents (although French is one of the major languages taught in our public schools).
>
> In all of the surveys and interviews I have conducted with staff and parents, the most prominent issue that has been brought up is the difficulty with communication. The parents state that their inability to speak English makes it extremely difficult to perform even the most basic of social tasks when English is required. Some also

state that they feel people equate their difficulty communicating with ignorance.

Not only are immigrants' communication difficulties often interpreted by others to be the result of ignorance, their lack of English frequently results in their children being misdiagnosed in school. The children are often mistaken for having learning disabilities, when the real issue is simply that they have not as yet learned to speak English.

Rory's investigation of how this issue manifested itself in his own center confirms this to be the case and reveals still other problems. An example is the story of Sekou, a child who was recommended for a special education evaluation because of his inability to follow instructions in class. Because Sekou was an English-language learner, Rory suspected that Sekou's learning difficulties had more to do with the child's limited English than any actual neurological or biological problems. Rory's sensitivity to this issue, and his efforts to secure the supports that Sekou needed to help him learn English, confirmed that this was indeed the case: as Sekou gained more mastery of the language, his learning problems became less of an issue.

As Rory was trying to make an appointment for Sekou's evaluation, he ran up against other difficulties commonly encountered by many immigrants. The problem began when dealing with the New York City Department of Education's well-intended regulation that student evaluations be conducted in a child's native tongue. The language in need of translation in Sekou's case was an African dialect called Joo-lah. Because there were no translators who spoke it in the Department of Education, Rory's center ended up having to pay one of the center parents who spoke that language to accompany the child and his family to the evaluation. In addition to the difficulties of convincing Sekou's busy parent to make the time to go through the tedious and somewhat intimidating process of traveling to and attending an official evaluation, Rory's center had to deal with the additional burden of paying for the cost of the translation because the Department of Education does not pay for outside translators. All of this vividly brought home to Rory how the language differences of many immigrants can be a barrier to their success.

Cultural Biases

The more Rory investigated the issues faced by his immigrant clients and neighbors, the more he began to realize that the center needed to change to adequately address their needs. And the needed changes had to do not only with language issues but also with a far deeper issue—that of cultural bias. To his surprise, Rory was learning that African immigrants faced discrimination not only from societal institutions but from the places and people of his own community as well. He explains:

As an educator and a community-oriented black American, one of my most surprising observations has been the way African immigrants have been treated or mistreated as they attempt to educate their children in Harlem. Even though this country's population is made up almost entirely of immigrants and descendants of immigrants who, in most cases, are more than happy to welcome and assist people from their homeland, I know that it is not unexpected or unusual for groups entering the United States to be met with resistance in the form of racism from ethnic groups other than their own. Surprisingly, in the case of these recent arrivals from the continent of Africa, people of African ethnicity [African Americans] often contribute to the barriers.

In my community, one that generally greets newcomers and their cultural idiosyncrasies with open arms, African immigrants are sometimes ridiculed for the way they dress and speak. Fun is made of their occupations, what they eat, and even how they smell. Sometimes they are encouraged to go elsewhere when they approach child care centers and schools in their own community.

Rory understands that these cultural biases are the reflection of deep-seated racial/cultural biases that extend far beyond the differences between African immigrants and American blacks. He sees these biases as being rooted in the narrative of the institutional racism that permeates our global society. The tensions between African immigrants and American blacks are simply the result of the fact that they live and work in close proximity to each other, a circumstance that presents more frequent opportunity for intermingling and thus more potential conflict between the two groups. Language is only a catalyst for these tensions. Rory's analysis of the situation is that each group believes the other group should do more to alleviate the problems:

Although both groups are of African descent, both bring different cultures, languages, or dialects to the host community. Each group feels that the other should learn [its] language. The African immigrant parents, according to my survey and interview responses, feel that even though we have a translator available at Harbor Morningside, other schools and institutions need to do so also. And the staff of Harbor Morningside, including two who themselves are African immigrants, feel the African immigrants have an obligation, as visitors in this country, to learn English. Neither group seems to have entertained the possibility of having an obligation to learn the other's language.

Other Forms of Cultural Discrimination
Through his interviews with parents in his community, Rory discovered that many immigrant families experience more problems than just com-

munication. Many feel that, although the language barrier between them and their host community is a major issue, they are victimized by discrimination even before a single word is spoken. They feel judged simply by their appearance. This has created problems for many immigrant families when they try to interact with schools in the community. Not only do they feel unwelcomed, but the atmosphere exaggerates what otherwise might be only minor difficulties. Ironically, the people who are prejudging, Rory observed, are often black Americans who live in the same community and are in the same socioeconomic bracket as the African immigrants.

Rory's readings about immigration theories and facts helped him gain a deeper perspective on the reasons for these tensions. While Africans and African Americans share similar experiences, their tensions are exaggerated by the fact that both groups experience racial discrimination. Rory explains:

> The institutionalized system of racial discrimination directed at [b]lacks in this country guarantees that both groups are likely to experience incidents of racial discrimination. Their living conditions alone are a prime example of this systematic discrimination. Schools, goods, and services in [b]lack communities are generally of poorer quality than in other areas. Most immigrants and migrants, whether they have professional skills or not, tend to reside in areas populated with large numbers of poor people and often lacking sufficient support services to meet the high health, social service, and employment needs of its residents.
>
> Much of the negativity between these two segments of the population is caused by a mutual lack of knowledge about each other's culture. Ignorance breeds fear and misunderstanding, which in turn, can create hostility and conflict. The bulk of both groups' preexisting knowledge of the other is often based on inaccurate portrayals in the media. Once they come in contact with each other, these

preconceived notions, along with language and other cultural differences, discourage positive interaction. African immigrants take offense at many Western cultural values while American [b]lacks often find it difficult to identify with immigrants since their ancestors were involuntary immigrants.[3]

PUTTING NEW UNDERSTANDINGS INTO PRACTICE

As a result of his investigation about immigration, Rory now has a deeper understanding of the issues that arise between different cultural groups. He sees the need to facilitate understanding and trust between them:

. . . Attempts must be made to bring the two groups together for the mutual benefit of a group of people who, though separated by distance and time, share the same ancestry and now share the same community. Although it sounds simple, it is no easy task. The misperceptions and pre-conceived notions are based on centuries of misinformation, some accidental, some deliberate. Both parties must take steps to understand, trust, and support each other.

Rory used this understanding to build on the intuitive efforts he launched when he first began as a child care center director:

When I became the director of Harbor Morningside my first priority was to create a sense of community. I very much believed in the philosophy that it takes a village to raise a child. I led by example, personally greeting all who entered the building, including the deliverymen. I began to refer to the staff, the children, and their families as "The Harbor Morningside Family." Everyone had a role in the task of educating and nurturing our children. Anyone who visited the center or offered support was inducted into the "Family."

Visitors were met with a smile and a friendly, sincere greeting. We had a tradition of taking the Harbor Morningside Family portrait once a year. All members of the Harbor Morningside Family were invited to be in it. The portrait was framed and displayed in the lobby of the building. All of this created a very warm and welcoming atmosphere.

Taking into consideration all that he learned about language and other cultural barriers, Rory worked hard to increase the diversity of his staff to reflect the cultures of the families in the center. He instructed them to be patient and helpful with clients who spoke little or no English:

Since language and cultural differences were a major issue, I hired people to work in the center who were from Africa. I hired a group teacher from Nigeria and two substitute classroom aides from Ghana and Senegal. I also increased the number of Spanish-speaking staff members when the opportunity presented itself.

Other changes that Rory made and that he recommends as a way to improve any community's relations were:

- Provide free or low-cost basic language courses for parents and staff as part of community outreach and staff development and encourage both groups to take part.

- Organize parent volunteers who speak languages other than English to create a pool of translators. Develop a funding source to pay them.

- Translate as much of the printed material as possible into English, Spanish, French, and, where possible, any other language spoken in the school.

Rory also created structures in his center to celebrate cultural diversity and make it a major part of the curriculum. One was an "open door" policy for his office that applied to staff, parents, and children. He welcomed everyone to approach him. Another was a "cultural education program" to help people learn about the many different backgrounds represented in the community. Town meetings and multicultural presentations enabled different groups to socialize with and get to know each other better, thus promoting greater understanding among them.

CHANGES

As these structures were put into place, people from all backgrounds within the center began to feel more welcomed and respected. And as word of the Harbor Morningside Family spread throughout the community, the population, which a few years earlier was made up mostly of blacks from the American South, transformed. After an initial sharp increase in the center's Latino population, a slow but steady rise in the African immigrant population led to the center becoming known as a welcoming place for African families. Its population, by Rory's estimate, grew to be ". . . approximately 75 percent African immigrants, 10 percent Latino, and 15 percent American [b]lacks."

REFLECTIONS

The tensions experienced in the center and the community between African immigrants and American blacks point to the importance of trying to see the world through others' eyes to truly connect equally as fellow travelers in the human community. How this can develop is illustrated in the following update of a children's story called the "Snow Kings" that Rory tells here in his own words:[4]

In the original story the three Snow Kings were white, black, and yellow. As it was retold in 1983, the kings were Hispanic, Native American, and black. For my purposes they will be black American, white American, and African immigrant. The story tells of three separate kingdoms surrounding and bordering an uninhabited area. The three kingdoms shared a great deal of mutual distrust and never associated with each other. It so happened that all three kings decided, at the same time, to explore the uninhabited area. They also all managed to fall into a pit at the center of the uninhabited area.

At first they all retreated to their own area of the pit and refused to associate with each other, but as time passed and individual resources ran low one king suggested that they huddle together to use their collective body heat to keep warm. Another pointed out that no individual was tall enough to climb out of the pit on his own and suggested that they stand on each other's shoulders to form a human ladder to reach the rim. When there was a natural reluctance to be the "bottom" section of the ladder, the third king suggested that he, being the strongest of the three, be the top of the ladder so he could pull the other two up once he reached the rim. They successfully freed themselves from the pit and returned to their kingdoms to make their reports and plan future joint explorations.

The lesson learned? The three kings, working together, were able to pull themselves out of the pit. They recognized that when people share the same problem and work at a solution together, none need lose his identity and all may benefit.

Ideas from Inside Rory's School

♦ It takes deep commitment and connection to a community to find the underlying causes of problems and to persevere in working out solutions.

♦ Lack of knowledge about a culture different from one's own can lead to fear and misunderstanding. Sensitivity workshops for the school community about the cultures represented in the school can be helpful in allaying such fears.

♦ Try to make sure that the school staff has representatives of the different cultural and linguistic backgrounds of the school's population.

♦ Plan multicultural events and projects that will enable different groups to socialize with each other. Through joint work they can gain greater knowledge and understanding of each others' cultures.

♦ Hold town meetings where problems and issues can be openly discussed.

♦ Provide free or low-cost basic language courses for parents and staff as part of community outreach and staff development and encourage both groups to take part.

♦ Organize parent volunteers who speak languages other than English to create a pool of translators. If possible, develop a funding source to pay them.

♦ Translate school informational material into the languages spoken in the school.

CHAPTER 9

Parental Supports for Early Literacy: Kisha Pressley

Kisha looked exasperated at the beginning of the year in her teacher research class as we discussed an article by a teacher in Kentucky who encouraged her kindergarteners to write using phonetic spelling techniques. The article's author describes how the principal and the students' parents became involved in an inspiring learning process. Kisha, who teaches prekindergarten in a school located in a Harlem public housing development, announced, "You know, I read this stuff and I think it seems so great, but I get frustrated because I know this just won't work in my classroom."

Kisha didn't believe that she would ever have the support necessary to make the Kentucky teacher's strategy work in her New York City classroom. She wanted to read about teaching that works in settings more like her own. The problem was that there just wasn't much currently available.[5] Most of the research literature she encountered seemed to focus more on the problems of urban students and families than on positive elements of their lives that could be used to enrich their learning. Frustrated with this state of affairs, Kisha decided to conduct her own study of teaching and learning with the children and families of her classroom. As will be seen in her story that follows, she not only was able to create a study that revealed positive elements of her community, but, through the process, she was able to broaden her own assumptions about what was possible in her work.

CONTEXT

In each of her classes over the years Kisha had always noticed a few children who entered school in September more advanced than their classmates. Although she knew that it is common for children to mature at different paces and in different ways, she wondered about what, if anything, in their home lives was responsible for the differences in their development. Driven by this curiosity, Kisha launched an investigation about what these particular children's parents were doing to support their learning.

Kisha's interest in this issue was very personal. Her mom had been in school only through the sixth grade and she was the first college and high school graduate in her family. Despite their limited educational opportunities, however, her family members instilled in her a strong belief that education is vitally important. Consequently, she did very well in school. Yet she always maintained a lingering feeling that her potential had not been fully realized. Given this background, combined with her interest in identifying strengths in urban families and communities that often are unnoticed by the dominant culture, Kisha had a strong interest in how parents who did not themselves have optimal educational opportunities could nurture children who are capable and excited about learning. She focused her study on how parents support the development of early literacy, a powerful emphasis in the schools as well as a strong predictor of academic success.

KISHA'S STUDY DESIGN

To begin, Kisha conducted a review of the research literature on literacy development—about how literacy behaviors begin, what is effective literacy teaching, and how parents can support their children's learning. Then she selected children to study who demonstrated high ability levels in communication, logical thinking, and reading and writing skills. She interviewed their parents, observed the children in school at various points of the day, and kept a journal that included reflections about her daily interactions with the children and their families.

From this data Kisha was able to create portraits of each of the parents (all mothers), which offered insights into why their children's development seemed to be so advanced. One mother, Karen, was a twenty-three-year-old single mom of two. Perhaps because she herself never liked school, Karen was intent on making sure that school would be challenging to her daughter. The second mother, Pamela, was thirty-five and a single mother of four. Living on her own since the age of thirteen, she gave birth to her son when she was only sixteen. Having completed her GED, she was in college working toward a degree in accounting. She was determined to do everything in her power to send her children to college as well. The third mother was thirty-eight-year-old Rosalind, a married mother of two. Rosalind had completed high school and was enrolled in a computer course at the time of the interview. She expressed regrets to Kisha that she had never gone to college.

WHAT KISHA LEARNED ABOUT PARENTAL SUPPORTS FOR LITERACY LEARNING

Kisha learned from her interviews that these three moms all provided at-home supports to enhance their children's learning: each made sure that there were ample learning materials in her home; each modeled a love of reading and created a literacy-rich environment; and each devoted considerable time to talking and playing with her children.

Providing Ample Learning Materials

In each home the children had their own bookshelves filled with many different kinds of books, and each mother made sure that she or other family members read to her preschooler on a daily basis. Karen, who was living on public assistance at the time of the interview, got her daughter's books as "hand-me-downs" from an older cousin. Whenever she was able to afford it, she purchased books that were relevant to their family's situation. For instance, when she was pregnant she bought an age-appropriate preschool book that explained how babies are born. She also bought chapter books that had no illustrations and frequently read them to her daughter to encourage her imagination. Both Karen and Pamela also provided books on cassettes for their children to listen to. In addition, all of the moms made other materials—such as letter magnets, alphabet blocks, regular wood blocks, puzzles, and other toys—available and accessible for their children to play with.

Modeling a Life Enriched with Reading

Rosalind, the most avid reader of the three mothers, was always reading books and magazines in front of her daughter, demonstrating the value and fun of reading. She also worked hard to instill in her daughter a respect for how to handle books. She confessed to Kisha that it made her crazy when she saw children mishandling books. Pamela, unlike Rosalind, was not a big reader, but her son, Carl, reported to Kisha that his mother was always doing people's taxes. Kisha explained that noticing his mother work on people's taxes "makes him aware of the function of reading and writing." And Karen, although not fond of reading books herself, always made them available to her daughter.

Talking, Listening, and Playing with Children

Each of the mothers whom Kisha interviewed spoke at length about the time they spent talking and playing with their children. Pamela, who had two older and two very young children, explained how she learned from her older children the value of spending time simply talking and listening to them. She explained, "The years went by so fast, me and the other kids really didn't have too much time to do anything. It was always work and school. Now there's more leisure time. We spend family time. My schedule allows it and I'm making a sacrifice to allow it. If I don't, then we are all gonna be fussing and arguing. I don't really like that." It was from experiences like these with her older children that Pamela learned the multiple benefits of talking things through and nurturing strong communication skills. She explained that she was "learning to try to listen" to her younger children's "whole story" so that they would become good problem solvers.

Likewise, Karen tried to nurture her child's language development and curiosity by watching television with her daughter so that she could be available to answer her daughter's ongoing questions about what she was viewing. "She asks questions and I answer them. She's been talking like this since she was one and a half." Karen also explained that she played Monopoly with her daughter to help her to strengthen her math and reasoning skills.

Rosalind described how she continually engages in conversations with her daughter: when her daughter pauses to ask questions as they walk down the street, when something is new, or when there's something she doesn't understand. Rosalind explained that she encourages her daughter to notice the words around them while they shop. She also tells her children stories about her own life to explain what she has been through and how much better things are for them than they were for her when she was a young child.

SHARING PARENTS' KNOWLEDGE

Kisha was astounded by how the mothers of her students intuitively knew about early literacy supports. She wanted to share what they knew with other moms and caregivers. So she developed a little printed guide describing the things they did that supported their children's learning. She felt it would be more helpful for parents/caregivers in her class to learn about how they could help their children at home from their peers rather than from outside experts:

> By using three parents in the guide who share the same culture and context as my future parents, I may be helping [other caregivers] to try some of the suggestions. If I can tell them that these are some of the techniques other single, working parents with "x" number of children have used to produce successful literacy, then they can feel confident that they can achieve the same results with their children.

When Kisha showed the guide to the director of her school, the director found the information to be so relevant that she immediately made copies of it for each child's family. Needless to say, Kisha was thrilled. She sent us an e-mail message that said, "I feel blessed and now I can't seem to stop researching things. One of the other teachers was helping me edit my paper. She is so excited she wants me to collaborate with her and conduct research on science and young children. . . ."

Through this process of conducting her own classroom-based inquiry, Kisha has found a way to bridge educational research with her own work. Her tacit understanding of the children's experiences has enabled her not only to investigate issues relevant to her setting, but also to highlight positive aspects of the experiences of her students and parents, thus providing an alternative to the deficit model of research about low-income families that she found to be so prevalent yet so limiting.

Ideas from Inside Kisha's Classroom

♦ Take the time to talk and listen to parents to gain understanding of what and how they provide learning opportunities for their children.

♦ Ask parents and caregivers to share their strategies for how they build literacy skills at home and then create a brochure, bulletin board, or newsletter containing the information.

♦ Help parents and caregivers recognize and value how they can use the environment (for example, reading signs, boxes from the grocery store, and license plates) as a tool for building literacy skills.

♦ Emphasize that playing and talking are important building blocks to literacy development: telling stories, playing games, asking questions, and listening to children are all important experiences for preschoolers.

Inside Differentiated Teaching

One teacher is usually responsible for the learning in a classroom of about twenty-five children. In some schools, especially urban schools, this number can be even higher. In one classroom there may be children who begin the year advanced in many areas of the curriculum while others are in need of tremendous support. The diversity of learning abilities, styles, and needs can range from children who need help understanding English, children who need assistance staying organized, or children who have special academic, social, or emotional needs.

How can a teacher provide an environment that ensures every child learns to the best of her abilities? In this section three urban teachers explore this question. Their stories offer a nuanced picture of the complexities involved in making a single classroom serve the needs of children who have many different kinds of needs. Neurys Bonilla presents an account of the challenges of teaching in a multiaged dual-language classroom, where students range in age from five to seven and have varying proficiency in two languages. Travis Sloane describes his exploration of how to differentiate his teaching to support the science learning of both "special needs" and general education students in a second grade classroom. And Carol Castillo shares her search for strategies that are effective in supporting the literacy development of the English-language learners in her kindergarten classroom.

Together, these stories demonstrate the careful work of effective teaching: observing and documenting how children learn as well as what they know and can do, reflecting on the information, and then adjusting instruction and shaping curriculum based on the new understanding gained. This ongoing cycle of assessment and teaching requires teachers who not only have solid content knowledge but also possess deep knowledge of how children learn, of how to collect and use evidence from children's work to make informed decisions about next steps for teaching, and of how to craft a curriculum that embodies needed knowledge and skills in a manner that is effective for each and every learner. This is highly skilled, nuanced work—very different from the commonly held conception of teaching as simply "delivering" curricula in a "one-size-fits-all" manner and then evaluating it through standardized tests that determine whether or not students will move on to the next grade. Teachers who possess these professional skills use knowledge of how people learn to shape and guide their teaching in ways that respond to the ever-changing needs of the children in their care. Teachers like these are effective at preparing students for the critical-thinking and problem-solving skills required for success in our twenty-first-century, globalized world. Their complex and complicated work is described in the stories that follow.

CHAPTER 10

Supporting Children's Diverse Needs
and Strengths: Neurys Bonilla

As a teacher of young children, Neurys Bonilla was accustomed to attending to the needs of the "whole child"—in other words, a child's social, emotional, physical, and academic needs. Because she teaches in a dual-language school (in which children learn equally in two languages), Neurys was already quite skillful at responding to students' individual variations and using these to support their learning. However, when she was asked to transform her dual-language kindergarten into a *multiage* dual-language classroom, in which there would be instruction in two languages with children more than a year apart, she felt challenged. The idea of having a group of five-, six-, and seven-year-olds of mixed abilities in the same classroom fascinated but scared her at the same time. Uncertain about her abilities to teach effectively to this wider age span, she nevertheless embraced her new responsibility as a great opportunity to grow as an educator.

The model for dual-language teaching in Neurys's school was "side by side," meaning that two classrooms shared two teachers, one responsible for teaching in English for half of the week and one for teaching in Spanish for the other half. Neurys was the teacher responsible for the Spanish instruction. The two teachers selected the students for their two classrooms. Including as many children as they could who had been in their kindergartens the previous year, they placed the children in the classes to ensure an equal balance between those who were English and Spanish dominant, those who were of different ages, and those whose academic abilities and social/emotional maturity varied within the two-year span.

Both teachers continued the child-centered teaching they had previously provided to their students. They maintained classrooms arranged in activity centers, in which students worked independently and in groups. The daily routines included times for individual work, student/teacher conferences, small group projects, and whole group activities such as morning meetings and "Author of the Day." A workshop approach was used for instruction in literacy, which means that children engaged in a variety of individual and small group activities to support the various aspects of reading and writing development. It was in this particular area that Neurys, because of the wide range of abilities displayed by her students, experienced most strongly the challenges of teaching children of different ages. She explains:

> The students who were at a higher academic level managed to engage in the process; however, it was a frustrating experience for students who were at a different stage. My anxiety level began to increase trying to find ways where I could give the younger students the time and space to grow while at the same time challenge those students who were at a higher level of achievement.

AN INQUIRY IS BORN

To help her figure out how to meet children's needs, Neurys launched an investigation into how best to support the range of learners represented in her classroom. She wanted to learn not only about how to most effectively advance everyone's academic development but also how to make sure that she did this in a way that created a sense of classroom community and left everyone feeling valued and recognized for their strengths.

To begin, she selected for study a group of nine students who represented the full range of abilities and ages (five to seven) in her classroom. Their levels of literacy development varied from those who were independent and fluent readers and writers to those who were at the earliest stages of literacy development. They also represented the gamut of social and emotional maturity among those in her classes.

Neurys observed her students in the classroom, keeping written documentation of her observations during writing, reading, math, and project times. Additionally, she collected samples of the children's work and took photos of them during classroom activities such as block building and dramatic play. This information gave her insight not only into the children's academic progress but also into how their social skills were developing. At the end of each day, Neurys reviewed her collected information, jotting down her reflections in a journal and analyzing what was going on. She used the understanding she gained from this process to identify her students' needs and strengths and design appropriate activities to guide their learning and challenge their abilities.

A New Awareness Emerges: Focusing Too Much on Difficult Behavior

As soon as Neurys began observing the children in her classroom, she noticed she was focusing too much attention, as is common for many teachers to do, on addressing the needs of those who exhibited the most difficult behavior (and who were often those who also struggled the most academically). This was brought to her attention by a girl in the class, who came to her one morning with the question, "*Neurys, porque tu siempre estas con Alejandro y Dina?*" (Neurys, why are you always working with Alejandro and Dina?) That question really opened Neurys's eyes. It made her see that, although the structures she had set up in the classroom were intended to provide time for her to work individually with every child, Neurys found herself unwittingly using these times to focus on the "difficult" children who needed more guidance. She realized that she was *over*addressing high-maintenance children at the expense of the others; that her attention to their negative behavior left her knowing little about their needs and strengths as well as the needs and strengths of the other, more well-behaved children in the class. This newfound awareness led Neurys to resolve to try harder to include in her focus *all* of the children.

Insights from Peer Tutoring

Peer tutoring is one of the most commonly used practices in multiage classrooms. Neurys tried this approach in the hope that it would challenge the high-achieving students in her class as well as support the development of the more reluctant learners. Pairing the students based on their reading and writing abilities, she grouped high-achieving students with those who struggled. When she first observed their interactions with each other, she noticed that the students were having difficulties interacting with each other. The high-achieving students complained about their tutees—that they were behaving negatively and were unable to sustain interest in the activities. The struggling students, on the other hand, resisted being supervised by a peer. Much of the time the pairs spent together was devoted to negotiating ways to solve conflicts and work together.

The relationship between Newton and his peer tutor Rosa offers an example of this dynamic. After working with Newton for the first time, Rosa complained to Neurys that he was not interested in learning. She told him, *"Como tu vas a apprender si tu no pones atencion?"* (How are you going to learn if you don't pay attention?) Newton responded, *"Tu no eres mi profesora."* (You are not my teacher.) In the course of three more sessions, however, the dynamic gradually changed between the two. Newton became intrigued with Rosa's ability to read, expressing an interest in learning from her. He asked her questions about how she learned to read and about the strategies she used when she confronted words she didn't know. Rosa, in turn, softened in her responses, finding ways to be less bossy and engage Newton when his attention strayed from the work. As a result of their relationship, the two children each modified their behavior and formed a bond with each other.

After a time, Neurys observed that, as a result of these peer tutoring relationships, the children gained a sense of interdependence and demonstrated a more caring attitude toward one another. They looked out for their tutoring partners during nontutoring activities, making sure that their friends were not in trouble and modeling effective learning behaviors for them. When the struggling students needed help in spelling, reading, or math, they looked for their tutors. During writing time, the pairs tended to work near each other. They often selected each other as partners for class trips or when they lined up during the day. Overall, Neurys found peer tutoring to provide students with opportunities to develop their academic abilities as well as such important social skills as interdependence, tolerance, and responsibility.

Recognizing and Responding to Students' Different Strengths

One strategy that Neurys used to ensure that she was adequately challenging the high-achieving students was to select high achievers to lead whole-class lessons. From trying this strategy she learned that she had previously too narrowly defined what "high-achieving" meant. What she found was that these children were uneven in their development: while many possessed advanced skills in one content area, the same children often were found to have less-advanced skills in other content areas.

For example, Neurys asked Eva, a proficient reader and writer, to lead a whole-class math activity. Even though Eva's writing skills were quite sophisticated compared to those of the rest of the students, she found herself having a difficult time leading the class through the math problem. Neurys noticed this when John, a child whom she had considered to be a struggling learner because he was in the earliest stages of literacy development, came to Eva's aid during the activity, demonstrating a sophisticated ability and confidence in his mathematical thinking. From this experience Neurys realized that her definition of "high achieving" was too narrow: that students were varied in their abilities and paces of learning in the different content areas and that being strong in one area did not necessarily mean that the same child was strong in all others. Neurys explains:

> As I observed students working on different tasks, I noticed that they have different levels of achievements in diverse areas. I also realized that their abilities do not always coincide with their ages. For instance, Newton and Rosa are the same age but have different reading and writing abilities. Dakelyn, who is much younger, has developed very sophisticated reading skills. John's writing and reading abilities are at the emergent stage, but he is able to use incredible strategies to solve mathematical problems. His understanding of mathematical concepts is what some people call "above grade level."

Recognizing this led Neurys to change the way she placed students into instructional groups. Instead of keeping them in the same group for the learning in all subjects, she started to vary how she grouped them. She sometimes created homogeneous groups for some subjects like reading, writing, and math when students needed to work on specific skills, but then made heterogeneous groups for other activities that drew on cross-disciplinary work, such as science, social studies, and project time. In homogeneous groups the instruction was based on students' demonstrated abilities at the time and the lessons were designed to address individuals' specific needs. For instance, Eva, Paula, Rosa, and Cecilia were placed in the same reading and writing groups. Because these students were fluent and independent readers, their reading group became a "book club" that focused on discussing the ideas of the literature. Other students who were not yet independent readers were placed in groups that read literature that was interesting but at a reading level that would challenge them to master the skills they needed to gain more proficiency as readers.

Heterogeneous groups of students were created for science, social studies, and research projects, all of which extended the study themes of the whole class. In such settings students had opportunities to collaborate and share their varying levels of understanding, to learn from each other, and to each develop a sense of accomplishment and responsibility. Organizing the children to work together in these ways confirmed for Neurys the need for teachers to provide a rich and diverse curriculum that fosters the growth of each student and is responsive to each child's needs.

NEW UNDERSTANDING LEADS TO NEW QUESTIONS

As a result of her study, Neurys became convinced that multiage classrooms provide opportunities to nurture both academic as well as social skills of students. She also learned that children's strengths and learning paces vary—that although they might be advanced in some content areas, they may be less developed in others. Mixing children together through peer tutoring, peer modeling, and flexible grouping supports their own unique pathways to academic growth as well as develops leadership skills, responsibility, and a sense of self-confidence.

What Neurys came to understand through her study is that the traditional dichotomy between "high-achieving" and "low-achieving" children is false. Rather, she became convinced that *all* children can achieve if they are provided with a rich learning environment that accesses their interests and special inclinations and supports their own paces of learning. This is what a good teacher does, whether in a single-age or multiage classroom.[1]

So Neurys came full circle in her thinking at the conclusion of her study. It led her to understand that good multiage teaching is really no different from good single-age teaching. Both require teachers to understand students and be responsive to their different learning styles, developmental levels, individual interests, and personal experiences.

This inquiry about multiage classrooms deepened Neurys's knowledge and convictions about good teaching. From it, however, new questions surfaced about the nature of our educational system: "But how can we [support children's individual strengths and learning paces] and grapple with the demands of an educational system that expects children to reach standards in a uniform manner? How can we respond to the demands of 'What every child should know by grade ____' if we know that it takes time for students to construct real knowledge?"

These new questions that surfaced from Neurys's study are complex. They may prove to be less answerable through her individual efforts than the original question she pursued, because they speak to many of the problematic ways that student success is conceptualized throughout our entire system of education—from narrow views of intelligence to a lack of appreciation for the diverse talents that people possess and the diverse ways that people learn.

In the years that have intervened since she began her investigation, Neurys has continued to wrestle with these questions. While she understands that she alone cannot provide a solution to many of the big-picture educational problems in our society, she *has* continued to confirm in the ensuing years that good teaching involves careful observing and documenting of students to get to know their strengths and needs, reflecting on the information collected, and using it to shape and guide instruction that is tailored to each and every child.

Neurys's ever-deepening understanding of teaching, as well as her increasing awareness of educational issues, has enabled her each year to better support the learning of her students so that, even in the limited ways that standardized tests measure learning, her students have been able to succeed. In this way, over time, she has helped countless children move closer to reaching their potential and realizing their dreams.

Ideas from Inside Neurys's Classroom

♦ Systematic observations of one's own teaching can lead to surprising revelations. When Neurys studied her own teaching she came to understand that her focus on the negative behaviors of challenging children got in the way of her ability to see their strengths.

♦ Peer tutoring can help students develop their academic as well as leadership skills.

♦ Collaborative work in heterogeneous groups presents opportunities for children to share their varying levels of understanding with each other, learn from each other, and develop a sense of accomplishment and responsibility.

♦ All children can achieve if they are provided with a rich learning environment that accesses their interests and special inclinations and supports their own paces of learning.

CHAPTER 11

Science Inquiry and Differentiated Instruction for Students with Learning Differences: Travis Sloane

Travis Sloane is a science teacher who was puzzled by how to help the students in his classes who were identified as having "special needs." In particular, he noticed a large discrepancy between the creative thinking these students were capable of when interacting with hands-on materials in the classroom and the labored, sometimes uninspired writing they produced about this work in their science journals. Travis wanted to figure out how to help these students transfer the knowledge, observations, and questions he heard them articulate when they were engaged in active learning experiences in the classroom to the written work they produced about it. He wanted to help them see and experience themselves as capable thinkers and learners.

Working with these struggling students led Travis to reflect on the experiences of friends from his childhood who had been in special education classes. One, who is now a successful comedy writer but who struggled in elementary school learning to read and write, particularly stood out in Travis's mind. This friend credits one of his teachers for contributing to his success in life because the teacher encouraged his self-esteem as a learner. Inspired by the story of how this particular teacher was able to build his friend's confidence in the face of great challenges, Travis became aware of the powerful impact a teacher can have in supporting a child's learning and changing his life. He committed himself to doing the same for his students.

LAUNCHING HIS INVESTIGATION

To begin, Travis launched an investigation to figure out how he could support struggling students to solidify their academic skills through the kind of active, inquiry-oriented learning experiences he knew best developed understanding of concepts.[2] He wanted to provide them with an alternative to the rote learning procedures and tasks that otherwise dominated their time in school. To do this, he explored literature on how to teach students with varying needs. Carol Ann Tomlinson's work on differentiated instruction was a particularly helpful guide. From it he learned that multiple entry points and multiple "sign systems" (ways of communicating—written, visual, auditory, etc.) should be available to help students learn; that through a blend of whole-class, group, and individual instruction he could use a variety of strategies to meet students' needs.[3]

Travis's teaching was also heavily influenced by the National Science Education Standards, a set of recommendations for science instruction put together by leading science educators. These standards emphasize a move away from lecture, text, and demonstration toward "guiding students in active and extended scientific inquiry."[4] They recommend teaching that is much like the way real scientists study the natural world: through investigations of natural phenomena that yield evidence and subsequently lead to explanations of how things work.

Focusing on a class of second grade students, which consisted of nine "special need" and sixteen general education students, Travis decided to study how he could use recommended active inquiry strategies with *all* of his students, regardless of their designated status and so-called "abilities." His plan was to investigate his teaching during a two-month study of rocks and soil, which he worked on twice a week with his students. His hope was to help them use their excitement about hands-on learning activities to develop their understanding of science ideas and to be able to present these in their written work. To do this he examined the lesson plans he created and videotapes he took of the children at work, along with the children's science journals and other related work.

EFFECTIVE STRATEGIES

From the evidence that Travis collected he was able to identify strategies that were effective at differentiating instruction for students with a range of needs. In what follows we share some of what he discovered about how to support his students' learning. We also describe how he supported the development of children's content knowledge through group experiences, how he helped children review key ideas from prior lessons, and how he strengthened his teaching by making it more inquiry-driven as a result of what he learned from his investigation.

Creating Study Tools to Support Children's Learning

Travis's study was motivated initially by his observations of his struggling students' participation during active, "hands-on" learning experiences. He noticed that in these contexts the students were engaged and made insightful obervations, but the task of having to document their thoughts in their journals seemed to deflate their initial excitement. He also noticed that for these students, setting up their journals was labor intensive; in fact, for some it took fifteen minutes to just copy the headings in the correct areas of the page. He felt that this time spent on copying and preparing journal

Figure 3.

pages was taking away from time that could have been spent on important scientific investigations. Still, Travis wanted the students to know that keeping a record of what they learned was an important aspect of being a scientist. To address this concern he created "observation pages" for them. The intention was to scaffold the experience of keeping a scientific journal so that his students could understand the essence of the experience without wasting their time on busywork.

Travis began the unit by having his students write their observations about rocks in their science journals. For second graders (many of whom were still at early stages of learning to read and write), this meant drawing

Figure 4.

pictures accompanied (sometimes) by descriptive words. The purpose of this activity was for Travis to assess how they would interact with this format and to see how the kids could describe their rock in their own words before they were taught the more standardized classification vocabulary. On examining the students' work, Travis saw that students wrote down their observations in simple words (see Figure 3). Many of them wrote one-word answers while some students wrote sentences describing what the rock felt like or what happened when they did something to the rock (see Figure 4).

After this activity, he had the class create a list of their descriptive words. Using this list, Travis created a work page that introduced different ways to categorize and compare the children's descriptions. He was not satisfied with his first attempt (see Figure 5) because he felt he hadn't provided a

Metamorphic Rocks

Rock # 1
Draw your Rock:

Shapes: □ △ ⬡ ═══ ○
Hexagonal

Colors:
White

Looks like: 👁
Small
Shiny

Feels Like: ✋
Soft

Rock # 2
Draw your Rock:

Shapes: □ △ ⬡ ═══ ○
Square

Colors:
Green
Black

Looks like: 👁
Hexagon

Feels Like: ✋
hard

Figure 5.

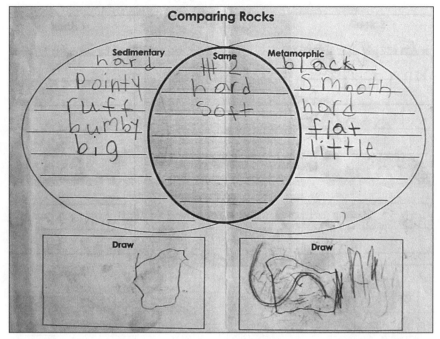

Comparing Rocks

Sedimentary | Same | Metamorphic
hard | #2 | black
Pointy | hard | Smooth
ruff | Soft | hard
bumby | | flat
big | | little

Draw

Draw

Figure 6.

structure to guide their thinking. This led him to develop another itera-
tion that provided visual organizers and picture cues intended to guide the
children as they compared and categorized the rocks (see Figures 6 and 7).

Travis made additional modifications to how the children used the vocabulary page too. Instead of just having them complete a worksheet describing the characteristics of rocks, he used real materials for them to work
with. For example, he found a striped rock and a bumpy rock, inviting the
children to handle them before filling out the form that asked for a description of the rocks' properties. This enabled the children to develop a real
sense of what the words meant and to more accurately describe what they
saw (see Figure 8). Throughout the rest of the rocks and soil study, as the

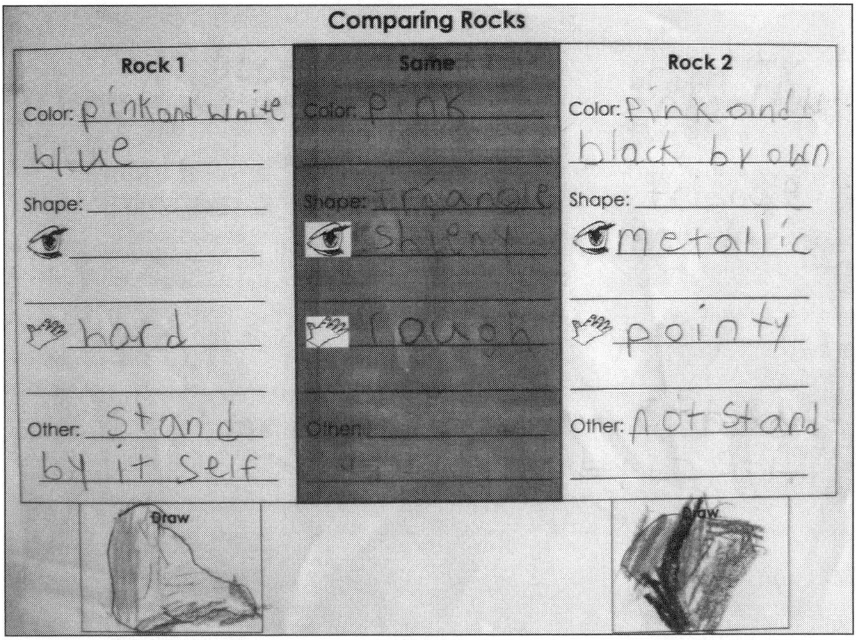

Figure 7.

children explored such topics as soil, water weight erosion, and sand dunes, Travis continued to provide them with real-life experiences and supported their thinking with worksheets that used similar written prompts and picture cues.

Using Group Experiences to Support the Development of Children's Content Knowledge

Travis was aware that learners understand new information best when it is presented in an experiential way and is connected to their prior knowledge and experiences.[5] He also realized that, among the students in his class, there were vast differences in the children's background knowledge. In order to avoid having situations in which only a few students knew much about

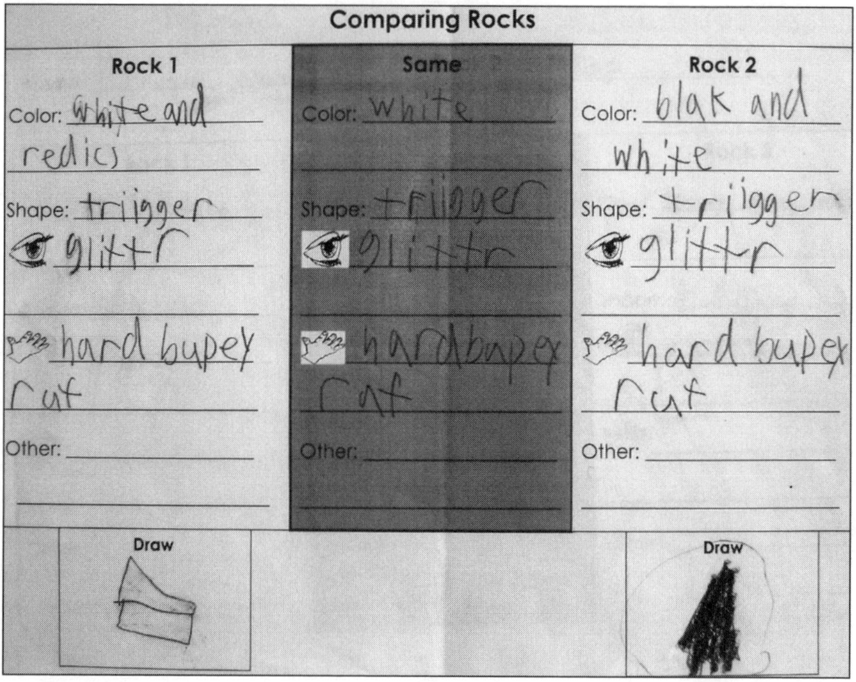

Comparing Rocks		
Rock 1	**Same**	**Rock 2**
Color: White and redics)	Color: White	Color: blak and white
Shape: triigger 👁 glittr	Shape: triigger 👁 glittr	Shape: triigger 👁 glittr
🖐 hard bupey rut	🖐 hard bupey rut	🖐 hard bupey rut
Other:	Other:	Other:
Draw		**Draw**

Figure 8.

the topic to be studied, Travis launched each study with some hands-on activities that all of the children could experience. In this way, he hoped that the students would have time to informally talk to their peers about their small discoveries and therefore have an opportunity to form a more equal foundation of knowledge for their subsequent explorations and discoveries.

For instance, when Travis first introduced the topic of soil, some of the children in the class had little experience with or knowledge about it. So he created an activity in which his students could explore soil in small groups. He gave each group three screens to use to sift soil, and they soon began to notice that it was made up of various sizes of pebbles, sand, and what the children called "soil" (not yet knowing the word "humus"). Next, Travis

Observing Soil (Outside)

Top of the Soil	Underneath the Soil
Colors:	Colors:
What does it look like? 👁	What does it look like? 👁
rock pencil soil store	Roteg 3 worms
What does it fell like? ✋	What does it fell like? ✋
vine Plant Rock brick	3 worms vine Plant dirt Soil
What other things do you see on the soil?	What other things do you see in the soil?
Sikes	Stikes

Figure 9.

took the class on a field trip to the school garden and placed students in partners to observe and write down everything they saw on the soil's surface. Then he gave them trowels to dig with and asked them to write about what they found. When they returned to their classroom the class made a chart and diagram of what was observed that day in their small groups and in partners (See Figures 9, 10, and 11 for a progression of work).

As a result of these activities almost all of the children in the class contributed to the construction of the class chart and diagram that kicked off the study of soil. Their concrete experience of "messing about"[6] with the dirt added to the understanding of all in the class as they embarked on studying soil in more depth.

Reviewing Materials to Build Stronger Understandings

One of Travis's concerns was how to help the children retain information from their studies. He was well aware that simply repeating activities did

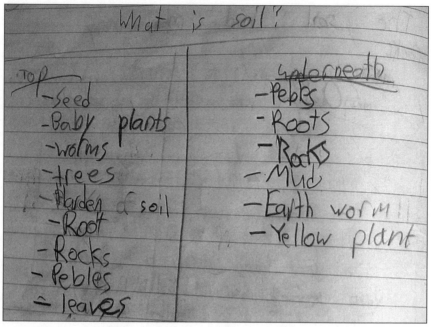

Figure 10.

not always support their understanding or their ability to hold on to that understanding. Through his investigation of his teaching, however, he came to see that repetition was helpful but needed to be combined with a variety of teaching strategies that connect to the learning styles of the different children. For example, he noticed that when the children observed a rock for a second time with guidance from one of his prepared study sheets, their descriptions became more developed. But the descriptions became even richer when Travis also provided the students with opportunities to share what they were learning in a variety of different groups. In one instance he found that by repeating the same activity first in small groups and then as a large group, students improved their understanding of the concepts. Additionally, Travis used other media and approaches to

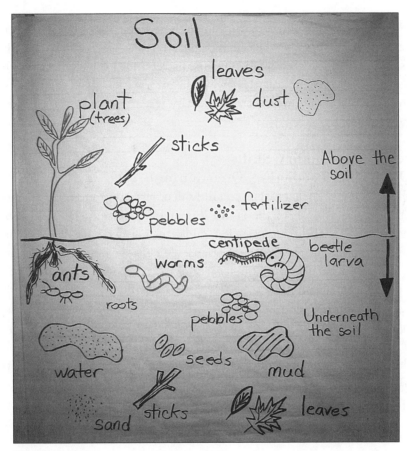

Figure 11.

enrich the children's learning. For example, when they were introduced to the three distinct types of rocks (igneous, sedimentary, and metamorphic), he shared with them a song that described how each kind of rock was made. Collaborating with the music teacher, he taught this "Rock Cycle" song to the class. As a result of working in these different ways, the students' understanding was strengthened.

Motivated by his success in working in these ways, Travis began to revisit previous units of study when he introduced new subjects to his class. For instance, when the class studied plants, he reminded the children of what they had learned about soil. Reviewing the information about soil from this new angle, he found, was another effective way to augment the children's understanding.

Developing Inquiry Skills
(Observing, Predicting, Questioning)

While Travis's students were certainly demonstrating more engagement with ideas as a result of the active learning explorations he was providing, he found that they still needed guidance and support in learning how to pose and pursue their own questions. To help them get better at these skills, he continually revised his teaching to incorporate even more of an inquiry-oriented approach.

In a lesson on water and wind erosion, for example, he offered many opportunities for the children to look at problems or questions, make predictions, and then find evidence to support the answers to the questions. The first activity he introduced to them on the topic involved showing the children a sand dune wind erosion tunnel. The model had a blue dune closest to the wind, then a green dune, and, farthest away, a white dune. First he asked the students to describe what they observed when the wind blew at their model of sand dunes. Then he asked them to predict the effect of water or wind on the materials: "If the wind blew again, what do you think would happen?" The children offered a variety of predictions: one wrote, "The blue sand dune was ompte [empty] and the green sand dune will be omst [almost] ampte [empty] and the yellow sand dune will be cover with all the sand."

Another day the class explored the topic of water erosion and experimented with water, soil, and a water erosion tub. As the children were looking at the soil and water, Travis asked them to predict what would happen if they poured a cup of water onto a dry area of soil. One answered, "The soil will be goopy." Later he asked what actually happened to the dry soil when they added water. The same student answered, "The soil turned to mud." Finally Travis asked the students, "What causes erosion?" The child looked at the evidence of her experiments and answered, "Rain causes erosion, making mud, and rivers, and waterfalls." She got it!

As the students engaged with the materials, Travis guided them to review their journals and observation sheets in order to develop evidence-based conclusions. He often worked individually with children who were experiencing difficulty. Through questions that probed the children's understandings and misconceptions, he was able to lead them to new understanding.

REVIEWING THE WORK

At the conclusion of the rocks and soil study, Travis reviewed the students' work. He was delighted to find that both the struggling and more proficient students had gained understanding of the study's content: the children were able to describe scientific concepts such as differences in rock structures and how rocks are made, soil composition and how soil is made, erosion, and the uses of rocks and soils.

Travis was pleased with the developments in his own teaching as well. He was especially pleased that he had provided the children with opportunities to work and think like scientists: while engaging directly with a variety of scientific phenomena, they developed their observing, predicting, and recording skills. As he reflected on the work, he saw the impact of the changes in his teaching on the children's attitudes toward learning: they clearly enjoyed working in an environment where they could freely explore their ideas and draw their own conclusions. His efforts to probe the children's thinking and to respond to their individual needs were critical, he concluded, to enabling those identified as having "special needs" to engage in the work and demonstrate their understanding.

Today, Travis continues to research his own teaching. As a partner in a National Science Foundation grant project to develop science curricula for K–5 students, he works with university professors and elementary teachers from schools all over the United States to develop and test methods and materials related to teaching for understanding. By his estimation, his research project has "enhanced and improved my overall teaching." By strengthening his own abilities to meet the learning needs of students with diverse abilities and skills, his investigation of his teaching prepared him for his current challenge. He now feels equipped to provide professional development to others on how to differentiate instruction and to mentor new teachers on how to begin the process of teaching using an inquiry-based approach.

Ideas from Inside Travis's Classroom

♦ It takes several drafts to create effective graphic organizers for students.

♦ To build a foundation for understanding new information, children need lots of "hands-on" opportunities to explore materials.

♦ When possible, provide students with visual references to help them understand and learn new vocabulary words.

♦ To help children retain what they are learning, repeatedly review the material with them, have them examine the information from different angles, and use multiple sign systems (like music or art) to develop stronger understanding.

CHAPTER 12

Supporting the Literacy Development of Young English-Language Learners: Carol Castillo

Carol Castillo teaches in a dual-language kindergarten in a public school in Washington Heights, an upper Manhattan neighborhood in New York City serving a large percentage of immigrant families from Dominican, Mexican, Ecuadorian, and Cuban backgrounds. Like Neurys's classroom described earlier, dual-language classrooms provide instruction that is evenly divided between English and another language, which in New York City is most often Spanish. Some classrooms have one teacher who instructs in both languages, while others have two different teachers who each assume responsibility for the instruction of one language. Carol is the teacher responsible for instruction in English.

Carol is uniquely suited for her position because she grew up in a family that spoke only Spanish. She understands the challenges of learning to read and write in English for children whose parents are unable to help them with their homework and who have difficulties communicating with school personnel. Because of this she is deeply committed to providing

English-language learners (ELLs)—sometimes referred to as "emergent bilinguals"—with the supports they need for school success.

CULTURAL AND CONTEXTUAL SUPPORTS
FOR ENGLISH-LANGUAGE LEARNERS

Carol knows that in order to foster English-language learning, schools need to recognize and appreciate the different cultures of their students, and they need to view the students' different backgrounds as strengths rather than "deficits." She also understands that teachers need to be familiar with the learning styles, communication patterns, and interaction styles that reflect students' different cultures and that they need to use multicultural materials in their classrooms to communicate that these differences are valued.[7] Toward that end, she tries to make connections with her students' families and the community to involve them in class activities and school life. She works to foster a sense of community in the class and create an atmosphere in which all children feel respected.

Another aspect of Carol's teaching that supports her emergent bilingual students is that she is adept at creating and maintaining a classroom environment perceived by students as safe, productive, supportive, and trusting. Having such a comfortable, stress-free environment helps language learners become fluent in their new language, because finding the right words to express themselves can occur more easily when they are in a relaxed, confident state of mind.[8] Krashen discusses the importance of creating a low "affective filter" (the emotional barrier created by fear, tension, boredom, or lack of interest) for people learning a second language.[9] Because Carol understands these issues, she tries to create "a home away from home" in her classroom to lower such anxieties for her young students.

To do this, Carol sees her role as teacher as including aspects of being a mother, a counselor, a mediator, a nurse, and a friend. She realizes, as the research indicates, that the relationships she develops with her students are critically important and can impact their participation in class activities, their work habits, their feelings about learning, and their peer relationships in school. She engages with her students conscious of the fact that teachers provide students with one of the most important "skills" that they will ever learn—that is, how to be in a relationship.[10]

In these matters pertaining to culture and classroom environment, Carol has generally felt confident. What she has felt less certain about, however, is her knowledge of specific teaching skills and strategies to help English-language learners learn to read and write. Because of this, she decided to pursue an investigation of how she could better guide and facilitate the literacy development of the English-language learners in her classroom. Her goal was to "make me a better, more insightful teacher in order to truly provide my students with the learning environment they rightfully deserve."

WHAT THE RESEARCH SAYS
ABOUT LANGUAGE ACQUISITION

Carol first did some background reading about English language acquisition. In doing this she discovered a widespread misunderstanding about emergent bilingual learners: that because they have developed English conversational skills, they therefore must have enough skills in their new language to learn academic content at the same pace as native English-language speakers.[11] What Carol's review of the research revealed is that English-language learners who are able to converse in English are far from having developed "cognitive academic language proficiency," a term first coined by James Cummins, meaning the ability to use their new language meaningfully in complex contexts, such as those in which academic content is taught.[12] Carol came across study after study presenting evidence that "English-language learners need five to seven years to master English well enough to work as proficiently in English as they can in their native

language."[13] Despite this knowledge from research, which is also confirmed anecdotally by many teachers, federal policies require that English-
language learners demonstrate proficiency on tests in English within a very
short amount of time. This contradiction between current policies and
what is known from the world of research and teaching puts educators like
Carol in the difficult position of having to prepare children to meet what
many consider to be unrealistic expectations.

LAUNCHING THE INVESTIGATION

To help her cope with this frustrating dilemma, Carol first combed the
literature on English-language learning in search of strategies for how to
teach and assess in ways that would enable her to best facilitate literacy
development for her students.[14] She then tried out these strategies in her
classroom, monitoring what she did and how she did it so that she could
figure out what would best meet the needs of the children entrusted to
her care.

Carol focused her study on six children in her classroom. While each
of these children had well-developed conversational skills, their literacy
skills, motivation, participation, and home support were varied. Carol explored her questions about these students by observing them in the classroom, keeping notes about the individual conferences she held with them
about their work, collecting samples of their writing and other projects,
and reviewing her regular assessments of their progress. She also maintained a personal journal that documented her reflections about her own
teaching—what worked, what didn't, and what ideas and feelings she had
about the challenges she was facing. Additionally, to broaden her understanding, she interviewed other teachers about what teaching strategies
they found to be effective in the classroom. She also surveyed the parents of her students in the hope of learning from them about how often
and for what purposes they utilized the English language as well as about

how much home support for English-language development they could provide.

EFFECTIVE STRATEGIES FOR TEACHING ENGLISH-LANGUAGE LEARNERS

As Carol combed the literature on teaching English-language learners, she was interested to learn that many literacy practices known to be effective for English monolingual children are also effective for English-language learners.[15] She was especially attracted to the Balanced Literacy approach,[16] which emphasizes teaching in the context of meaningful, purposeful activities rather than teaching skills in isolation (through worksheets and drills). She was drawn to this approach because it confirmed what she knew about how young children learn: that they retain information and skills best through active, contextualized experiences.[17]

Explicit Teaching and Modeling

When Carol began to examine what helped her students learn how to read, her experiences confirmed what she had read about in the research literature: that they best learned to recognize and understand words in print in the context of reading real literature rather than by memorizing vocabulary lists or being drilled on sounds and symbols. However, she also came to see that some skill learning did not happen by itself—that strategies needed to be explicitly taught and modeled. For example, when Carol read with an ELL child and that child came across a word he did not recognize, she often needed to demonstrate to the child how to search for a known word within the unknown word—for example, "old" within the word "mold."

Another teaching approach that Carol came to realize is helpful for supporting English-language learners is to explicitly model strategies and techniques using children's literature or their own writing. When she did this for them, abstract concepts came alive. For example, when Carol demonstrated to her class how to identify the "beginning, middle, and end" of a story, this gave them guidance for what to do when they were asked to complete a similar assignment. And when she demonstrated to Alejandro how to find a "just right" book (one at just the right difficulty level for independent reading), he "got it" and subsequently began to use this technique on his own during independent reading time.

The more explicitly she guided her students in the context of their daily activities and the more she provided opportunities for them to be exposed to and engage with the English language—through listening, speaking, reading, and writing—the more they learned and the more adept they became in their language use.

Individualized Teaching

Working with children individually and in small groups was another approach Carol found to be helpful to her English-language learners. Each day in her classroom she provided time for children to work independently in different activity centers. This made it possible for her to work with individuals or small groups in order to tailor instruction to their needs. It was during "center time" that she provided experiences for children to work on a needed skill or technique. She figured out the skills the children needed by examining their written work as well as by reviewing the documented observations she took of them in the classroom. For example, because her records indicated that Ernesto was having some trouble recognizing the difference between the letters "b" and "d," she assigned him to work in a small group on activities that involved identifying the beginning sound of words. The children worked on this skill by looking at picture cards and selecting the beginning letter from several listed beneath the picture. Because each picture card had the word describing the picture on the back, the children could do this activity independently, without direct teacher instruction. They talked together during these games, which enhanced their English conversational abilities. And during this process, freed from "directing" their every move, Carol was able to observe the children, which yielded valuable insights for her about the ways they approached learning, their interests and strengths, as well as areas in which they could use further support.

Word Wall

Using a "word wall" was yet another teaching strategy that helped to support English learning in Carol's class. A word wall is a chart displayed on a classroom wall of alphabetically organized words that students have come across during conversations or group readings. The word wall is a reference tool that children can use when they are reading or writing. It is useful because the children can refer to it independently to check on their spelling or to find a word that they want to use. Carol's teaching journal documents some of the ways that a word wall can support children's literacy development:

> Cumba is really improving in her writing. I noticed that using the word wall has really increased her confidence when she is writing sentences. Today during writing time she finished her work and then called me over so she could read it to me. Although she had some words phonetically spelled [another important strategy for learning the sounds of letters and words], she had all the words that appeared on the word wall spelled correctly on her paper. I asked her how she knew how to spell "flower" and she said she got it from the word wall.

Rhythmic, Rhyming, Repetitive Texts

Another discovery Carol made through her investigations is that English-language learners, just as is the case with all young readers, respond best to texts that have rhyme, rhythm, and repetitive language. She found that these kinds of texts helped the children to decipher the print as well as to understand and be involved with the story. Reading such books to her class was so helpful that Carol began to include more and more of them during the read-aloud times she had with her class.

Noninstructional Support

In the course of her investigation, Carol came to a powerful realization: that noninstructional, informal activities are a powerful means by which to develop children's literacy in English. She noticed that when children were engaged in chants, songs, and rhymes in the classroom, their verbal expression was enhanced. But even more powerful, Carol came to see, was getting the children involved in trips, dances, and other play activities. In such experiences, the children were so engaged and excited by what they were seeing and doing that they couldn't contain themselves from sharing their thoughts. Lively conversations seemed to explode and accelerate their language learning, which also carried over to their literacy skills. A trip to the Bronx Zoo brought this point home. The children's excitement about the experience stimulated conversations. This, in turn, enhanced their vocabulary, revealing all the knowledge and information they were acquiring. As she listened to them animatedly talk about the animals they had seen and which one they liked best, Carol overheard Ernesto tell Alejandro that "the snake is dangerous." Alejandro responded, "Not if it's in the cage. But anyway, I like the peacock better. It's so pretty." When Ernesto turned to Carol and asked her how to spell the word "peacock," she was reminded of how effortless talking and writing can be when they flow from an interesting activity. And she began to understand in a whole new way how involvement in rich activities feeds children's vocabulary and expressive development.

Reflecting on this later, Carol recalled the children's eagerness to talk about what they had experienced. "The vocabulary literally flowed out of the children as they expressed what was meaningful to them," she said. "It was then that I decided to try to include more open-ended activities and play in my classroom and to observe carefully what impact it had."

After observing the children carefully during these times, Carol came to another important realization:

As I view the children in the different areas, creating and talking to one another, I have come to realize that all the units of study that these children have to complete could easily be done through their play. I look at the children on the rug working on building a train as they tell each other where they are going on the train. Bam! That's an instant personal narrative. They are showing each other how to build the train (this could be a "how-to" book). At the other corner of the room John is making pizza out of clay (another "how-to" book). I could go on and on.

Recognizing the powerful impact that informal experiences can have on promoting language and literacy development, Carol has since provided more time in her classroom for open-ended activities and play. As a result of her study, she is now convinced, more than ever, that trips and other active experiences must be a part of early childhood classrooms. Her investigation confirmed to her that when children are given the opportunity to choose their activities and to learn through experiences, their thinking, their language, and their literacy abilities blossom.

ASSESSING STUDENT LEARNING: A CRITICAL PART OF TEACHING ENGLISH-LANGUAGE LEARNERS

Carol arrived at her understanding of the importance of active learning through her careful observations of the children at work in her classroom. These observations helped her to carefully monitor their academic progress. She documented and dated her observations to make the children's daily progress visible. Additionally, she saved and carefully reviewed their work, which gave her information about how their skills and knowledge were developing. These assessment practices gave her information that she didn't get from standardized tests. They helped her to see each child's different and preferred ways of learning, which, in turn, she used to guide her decisions about how to shape her instruction to make it more effective.

For example, from her observations of Evelize during story time, Carol came to see that Evelize responded especially well to texts with rhythmic, repetitive lines. These kinds of books held her attention and helped her to grasp the meaning of the story. Carol's recognition of how Evelize worked led her to use more of these kinds of texts to help Evelize move forward with her reading.

Conferencing

Another way that Carol monitored and supported the literacy development of her English-language learners was to hold individual conferences with them. Working with the children one-on-one helped her learn what they understood and what they didn't, what they could do and what they struggled with, as well as what strategies they used in their learning. For example, conferencing with Alex about the book he was reading led Carol to discover that even though the book was at the right difficulty level for him to read it independently, he wasn't really reading it; he was just looking at the pictures. Noticing this led Carol to model for Alex strategies he could use to decipher and make sense of the text. In this way Alex acquired the skills needed to complete his book independently.

Carol's experience with Alex, along with similar ones with other children in the class, confirmed to her that assessing children and their work is an important support for English-language learners: "Conferencing helps to identify what the student knows and does not know. It is an opportunity to write and keep note of when the teacher conferred with the child and what was discussed so that when the teacher sees that child again he/she will know if the student has made any progress and where to begin. This form of monitoring allows the teacher to gather information about each individual student, helping the teacher plan how to best guide the students."

CONCLUDING THOUGHTS

As Carol examined the information she collected from her study, she noted that her students developed literacy in English through a variety of approaches. Her investigation of the research on English-language learning and of how she was incorporating this knowledge into her teaching showed and reassured her that she was doing many of the recommended practices: explicitly teaching strategies and skills in the context of meaningful, purposeful activities; modeling these strategies for her students; conferencing with students; and using the information she gained from assessments (such as observations and reviews of student work) to help her understand each child's needs and use what she understood to shape her instruction.

The biggest revelation of her study, however, was Carol's discovery of the power of the "noninstructional" learning that took place in her classroom. She explains:

When I began this study I knew that chants, songs, and rhymes were effective in teaching English-language learners. The readings and the ESL (English as a Second Language) teachers I interviewed confirmed that these teaching methods had been effective throughout their years of teaching. However, what I found to be much more interesting was how other forms of noninstructional approaches affected the literacy development of my English-language learners. I found that dance, class trips, and, most important, play helped to create a stress-free environment where students felt comfortable and confident to express themselves. Play is an excellent venue to support children's learning. Learning literacy in another language through play is no exception. Play can help foster language learning easily and effectively and my study is a good example of how that happens. The research literature that I read, in my opinion, did not place enough emphasis on this.

When I review my observational notes on children at play in the classroom, I see the students almost transform into creative talking machines. During the times when the children played in the classroom I noticed how they applied literacy skills, math skills, social studies, and science skills without actually having to isolate them into separate categories. I noted instances where the students were telling stories based on the objects they built with the blocks. They counted the number of blocks they used and sometimes created patterns. Many created scenes of their day at home and talked about it.

I was amazed at what they can do and learn through play and I can go on and on about it. Having witnessed these advantages that play has to offer children who are learning a new language, I will try in the future to advocate for it to be more prevalent in the early-childhood curriculum in my school. I can easily demonstrate how the work the students produced through play is aligned with the curriculum and state standards. I will continue to implement play in my classroom whenever I can until the administration sees the value of this teaching in this way and integrates it into the school curriculum.

CHANGING TEACHING, CHANGING THINKING

Carol's study of how to support the language and literacy development of English-language learners had an impact not only on her teaching but also on her thinking about herself. She admitted that before she began her investigation she was always worried about meeting the expectations of the administration. Through her inquiry, however, she affirmed that the strategies she had been using with all of the children in the class were helpful to her ELL students as well. She not only strengthened her knowledge base and added to her repertoire of effective teaching skills but also gained a sense of confidence and pride in being a professional, taking charge of her own learning and her work:

> I used to think about how I would get the students to do what the administration wanted them to do. Now my thinking has totally done a turnaround in that I think about how the work the students do fits into what the administration wants them to do. As a professional, before I began the study, I felt as though I was being told what to do and what to say. Now, having had the opportunity to carry out this study, although the curriculum I am required to teach is still a scripted one, I feel more in control of my teaching. I feel strong enough to decide how to teach it and to take into consideration where the students are, what they need, as well as what I expect from them.
>
> As I continue to reflect on my teaching I also see the importance of questioning what I do. Being able to ask myself what I think is going to work and being able to try it as well as observe the outcomes has strengthened my teaching. Not only am I amazed by the work my students have done, I am much clearer now about how they did it. This research study has really helped me to better understand good teaching. I will always keep in mind that each student learns differently and that my job is to teach to each learner.

Ideas from Inside Carol's Classroom

♦ English-language learners need five to seven years to master English well enough to work as proficiently in English as they can in their native language.

♦ Informal experiences such as open-ended activities, classroom trips, and opportunities to play can have a powerful impact on promoting language and literacy development for early-childhood students.

♦ Teacher assessments, such as careful systematic observations and conferencing, are vital in assessing ELLs' academic growth and aiding the teacher to understand what academic supports are needed for the child.

Inside the Constraints of Urban Teaching

At all grade levels, high-stakes testing has had a considerable impact on the day-to-day lives of schoolchildren and their teachers. In this last section of our volume we share three urban teachers' explorations of how to deal with constraints in their schools that are influenced by national, state, and district policies. Hazel Veras-Gomez, a kindergarten teacher, investigates how she can provide more time for her students to engage in active learning experiences within the constraints of the demands imposed by her school's mandated curriculum and standardized testing. Prekindergarten teacher lisa schaffner (her preferred spelling) explores how, despite academic pressures trickling down from the upper grades, she can include more time for physical activity in her students' daily schedule. And finally, Laurie Jagoda, a middle-school teacher, seeks to find ways to keep her school's emphasis on aligning curriculum with state standards and preparing students for standardized tests from overwhelming the culture of the school.

Despite the constraints these teachers face, they have found ways to create productive learning environments in their classrooms and schools that are responsive to their students' needs. Although their road to change hasn't always been easy and hasn't led exactly to where they expected, their inspiring stories offer images of possibility for how teachers lead and bring about needed improvements in schools.

CHAPTER 13

What Is Happening to Our Children's Garden?: Hazel Veras-Gomez

After working as a pre-K teacher in a day care center for several years, Hazel Veras-Gomez was excited to acquire a position as a kindergarten teacher in a public elementary school in Washington Heights, a diverse neighborhood in the northern corner of Manhattan's West Side. Nearing the completion of her master's degree in early childhood education, Hazel was keenly aware of the research on the importance of play in young children's development, and how it helps children interact with peers, problem solve, and build foundational literacy and cognitive skills—all of which are critical prerequisites for successful engagement in more abstract academic work.[1] She was eager to apply her newly acquired knowledge of child development to the classroom so that she could provide the kind of active learning/play–based experiences that she has come to understand are most appropriate for advancing the learning of young children.[2]

THE PROBLEM

Hazel was surprised and dismayed to find out that the kindergarten she was asked to lead was very different from the kind of environment she considers to be appropriate for children of that age. Instead of being a "garden" where children are introduced to "big school," filled with opportunities for playtime, music, nap time, making friends, and, best of all, just being a kid, it was much more academic than the child-centered environment that she had learned was best for kids and that she remembered experiencing as a child:

> As I reflect on my own kindergarten experience, I remember a warm feeling of acceptance; a home-away-from-home sort of feeling comes over me. I remember playing, socializing, nap time, and doing fun activities through art and music. But kindergarten has undergone dramatic changes since then. Play is no longer an important part of the kindergarten curriculum. Instead, kindergarten children and teachers are faced with increasingly demanding academic mandates. It seems as though the children are really in the first or second grade. As I teach, I find it really hard to believe that these five- and six-year-olds are experiencing such academic pressures. As an early childhood educator, I feel the pressure and I'm caught between the mandates and my professional beliefs of how I want to teach and how children should learn.

Hazel thus began her first year of teaching kindergarten feeling a bit overwhelmed and filled with questions. She wondered: How do the changes in kindergarten affect children's social/emotional development as well as their cognitive development? How do these changes impact children who are experiencing school for the first time? And she asked herself: How can teachers meet the demands of the curriculum imposed by the district and still teach in developmentally appropriate ways that meet the needs of each child? How would she be able to make time for centers or free play given all the structures she was told to follow and the requirements she had to meet in her classroom?

Bravely, Hazel decided to use her dilemma as an opportunity to advance her learning. She resolved to examine the issue of how to make time for developmentally appropriate practice in the context of the curricular constraints she faced. To do this she decided to keep a journal that recorded her teaching experiences and her observations of her class. She also took pictures of events in her classroom and interviewed other teachers in the school to learn about how they attended to their students' needs while still handling the curricular demands placed on them.

As a result of her investigation, Hazel confirmed that, indeed, kindergarten is no longer considered a grade where children are expected to enjoy rich, active learning experiences. Rather, it has become more of a mini–first grade, filled with academic demands, paper-and-pencil tasks, and very little time for play, not what she had remembered it to be or what she had learned in her own schooling was appropriate for young children. Her study of this issue documented some of the ways that current kindergarten practices are pushing children to do more than they are developmentally ready to do. It also recorded the impact of this phenomenon on the children in her classroom. What she learned helped her generate ways to bridge the competing demands of school requirements with the natural ways in which young children learn.

IDENTIFYING THE PROBLEMS

Through her study Hazel identified several aspects of life in her kindergarten that got in the way of her students' optimal learning.

No Room for Play and Active Learning

One problem was that there was very little room in the required daily schedule for the children to have active learning experiences. The day was mandated to be very structured with every period designated to paper-and-pencil work in a specific academic subject. While she wanted her students to have a time when they could engage in more playful types of learning, on some days there was so much to do that there simply was not enough time for it. (Figure 12 shows a typical daily schedule in Hazel's classroom.)

Big chunks of each day were supposed to be devoted to the Reader's and Writer's Workshops, times for reading and writing organized around a monthly unit mandated by the school. When the time came for the required unit to be "nonfiction," Hazel had a lot of ideas for how to gear the work to the children's interests and for how to provide the children with active, real-life experiences (like field trips) that could help them understand and relate to the abstract concepts and information presented. However, when she shared these ideas with the other teachers and the supervisor of her grade, she was told that field trips were not allowed. Hazel was disappointed by this response because she felt that taking trips could be a way to bring the ideas to life and thus strengthen the children's understanding.

A Long School Day

Still another problematic aspect of her kindergarten class, Hazel soon realized, was the fact that the school day was very long. In addition to the length of the regular school day, an additional thirty-seven and a half minutes had been added on, mandated by the district for basic skills teaching in preparation for standardized tests. This "extended day" time made the school day almost seven hours long, during which time the children had little opportunity to move about, take a rest, or eat. With lunch scheduled at 10:30 in the morning in order for the school to be able to accommodate the large number of classes that needed to use the cafeteria, and with no snacks provided by the school throughout the day, the children often got hungry, restless, and tired by midday—not the most optimal conditions in which to learn. Hazel felt strongly that they needed to have rest and food

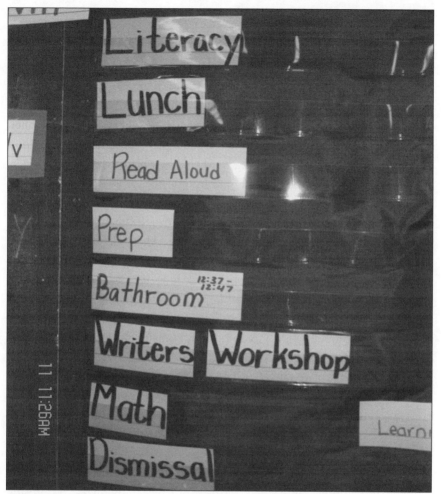

Figure 12.

to keep their energy levels up. She also felt that they needed some time for play-based experiences to support their cognitive, social, and emotional development.

Too Much Testing

Another element of kindergarten that gave Hazel cause for concern was the amount of testing required throughout the school year. Some tests mandated by the district yielded little information that she found useful to her teaching, yet they took inordinate amounts of time to do. And then there were still other tests—end-of-unit evaluations—also required by her school. These too gave Hazel cause for concern because her observations of the children during the testing confirmed to her—which she already knew—that paper-and-pencil tests are limited measures of what children know and can do.[3] An incident that offers evidence of this took place one day when Hazel noticed Alfonsina sitting at her desk while taking a test with a troubled look on her face. When she asked the child what was wrong, Alfonsina began to cry and explained that she could not identify the word "come"—one of the "high-frequency" words that the children were expected to commit to memory—in order to fill in the bubble under the correct spelling. Hazel knew that the child could recognize and spell this word in context and that her ability to do this could easily be confirmed through observations and examinations of the child's writing.

Experiences like these helped Hazel understand, in a deeper way than ever before, why early-childhood and psychological professional associations, as well as many other educational experts, have long opposed standardized testing for young children. She had firsthand evidence of how limited standardized testing is in revealing children's skills and knowledge, of the stress it can produce, and how it can negatively affect children's perceptions of themselves as learners and as competent individuals.[4] As a result Hazel was firm in her belief that "there is no need for five- and six-year-olds to be so stressed over a unit test to break down and cry. As an early-childhood educator, I must find a way to help my students feel confident and to reassure them that it's okay if they don't know."

VETERAN TEACHERS AGREE

Hazel was not alone in experiencing these problems of kindergarten that she was documenting. When she interviewed other kindergarten teachers, they too gave examples of the pressures they were experiencing to teach in inappropriate ways, despite their concerns that the curricular demands were harming children's social and emotional development. One teacher noted that because standards have to be met within a given time frame, she is not able to support children to develop at their own pace (a long-honored principle of early-childhood teaching) and that, because of this, she feels her kindergarten curriculum is not adequately meeting children's needs. She complained that the kindergarten classroom she is required to maintain is "completely skipping some of the basic stages necessary for academic, social, and emotional development." And because of this, she explained, the children become frustrated and/or bored, which then causes discipline problems to occur.

The final straw for Hazel, however, was when one day she read a book to the class called *Miss Bindergarten Gets Ready for Kindergarten.*[5] At the end of this book the children in the story have the opportunity to paint, build with blocks and other materials, and get involved in dramatic play. When Hazel came to that part of the story, one of the children in the class asked, "How come we can't have playtime like that?" Hazel's heart nearly broke. It was then that she resolved to do something to end what she felt was her complicity in depriving children of their right and need to play.

MAKING CHANGE

As a result of what Hazel learned from her close examination of what goes on during the course of the kindergarten day, she took steps to make changes in her classroom so that she could be more responsive to children's needs. First, she carved out room in the afternoons so that they could have some time for more active, play-based learning experiences in the different centers of the classroom. She did this by reallocating time away from the rigidly structured activities of her math, reading, and writing times. Observing the children as they sorted and categorized numbers and shapes while building with blocks, as they explored the properties of bubbles at the water table, as they kept journals of their investigations in the science area with soil and insects, as they engaged in animated discussions in the dramatic play area, and as they began to understand language structure and syntax while drawing and writing in the art area, she saw how much more interaction, socializing, and dealing with each other's emotions took place through play; how much more meaningful learning was going on; and how many more children were better able to learn and express their learning through these active, generally thought of as "nonacademic" experiences than through the largely paper-and-pencil tasks that took up so much space in the mandated curriculum.

Hazel took yet another step to support her students by addressing the fact that they got really hungry during the day. After deciding to provide a snack time in the afternoon so that the children would have something to eat during the long extended school day, she sent a letter home to all the families asking them to pack their children's backpacks with something healthy for their children to eat. This helped considerably to sustain and support the children's energies and learning efforts.

And finally, Hazel worked to figure out how to adjust the mandated curriculum to be more appropriate to her students' developmental levels. For example, when doing the required nonfiction unit of study mentioned earlier (for which she had suggested taking trips but was told this wasn't allowed), Hazel fought off her feelings of being overwhelmed by the requirement to produce books with tables of content, indexes, and glossaries, and, instead, conducted the study in a way that was appropriate to the children's understanding and was connected to their interests and skills. She turned the unit into a study on "All About Our School," which involved a series of experiences that included taking the children on a tour of the school and on visits to the homes of different students in the classroom. The class then subsequently used their experiences and the pictures they took during their visits to write and put together their own books. Included in the books were the unit's required components. In this way, Hazel created a project that complied with the curriculum while at the same time being child-friendly and child-oriented.

As Hazel became more familiar with the school requirements, she got better and better at adapting the curriculum to the children and their developmental needs. Reflecting on what she did and the changes she made, she was pleased that she took matters into her own hands to ensure that her teaching was tailored to how children learn. She noted, "I think I just listened to my heart and common sense and just went with it. I let my knowledge of children's development guide me."

This study of her kindergarten classroom helped Hazel find a way to build bridges between where the children were developmentally and the school's requirements. Although she still regretted that her class was not getting the full amount of time for play that she believed they needed, Hazel's actions on the children's behalf *did* result in an improved learning environment and a good beginning for her to continue to learn even more about how to be creative and better manage to fulfill academic requirements in developmentally appropriate ways.

REFLECTIONS ON GROWTH

As Hazel looked back on her first year of teaching kindergarten in a public school, she realized that she had accomplished a lot. Through her research she found evidence that kindergarten children are increasingly faced with academic pressures regardless of where they are developmentally.[6] At the same time she also found evidence of how important play is to children of kindergarten age, confirming what she intuitively had known all along:

that powerful learning happens through play and needs to be a big part of kindergarten life.

Because Hazel's study focused not only on identifying problems but on examining ways to address those problems in her teaching, she found that it helped her to figure out innovative ways to balance the curricular demands set forth by the Department of Education with what she knew was best for children's learning. The whole process of examining, reflecting, trying things out, and reflecting on her work yet again gave her confidence that she, as a professional, could successfully find ways to resolve, or at least move forward with, some of the challenges and dilemmas encountered in teaching.

From this experience Hazel took away a renewed sense of power and trust in her knowledge of what supports children's learning. She also gained some concrete strategies for how to retain some of the spirit of the "garden" upon which kindergarten practices were originally based. She expressed these revelations in her journal notes at the conclusion of her study:

> This has been a learning experience for me in more ways than one. I have learned to trust myself and follow my instincts when it comes to the students I am responsible for. As an educator, I now realize that meeting the needs of our children and doing so in developmentally appropriate ways is the key to reaching our children and making a difference, despite what mandates we are facing or what deadlines we need to meet. The bottom line is that our children are getting lost in the world of mandates. We have to make changes and put our children first.

Ideas from Inside Hazel's Classroom

♦ Despite the current focus in many schools on curriculum mandates and testing, teachers can develop concrete strategies for how to meet children's educational needs in the early grades.

♦ Some effective strategies are:

  • Creating time in the school day so that kindergarteners can have time for active, play-based learning in the different centers of the classroom.

  • Eliciting the help of families in providing a snack to help children maintain their energy throughout a long school day.

  • Finding ways to meet the expectations of district and state standards by adapting curriculum to children's developmental levels, interests, and needs.

CHAPTER 14

Incorporating Physical Activity into the Public School Prekindergarten Day: lisa schaffner

lisa schaffner[7] is a veteran prekindergarten teacher at Central Park East II Elementary School. This small public school in East Harlem, founded in the 1970s by the now-renowned educator Deborah Meier, provides children of diverse cultures and backgrounds with active learning focused on the needs of the "whole child." Even in such an environment, however, lisa had serious concerns about whether her students were getting enough physical activity. She worried about how the school system's current emphasis on high-stakes testing has led to increased pressures to provide paper-and-pencil work for younger and younger children at the expense of recess and other play-based activities. She worried as well about how children's lives are increasingly being dominated by video games, TV, computers, and smart phones, causing them to be so sedentary that our nation is faced with an epidemic of childhood obesity.

lisa always considered herself to be a "not very physical person." Running, climbing, and jumping did not come to her naturally, and, she remembers as a child shunning organized games and sports. However, as the parent of a New York City public school child and as a teacher committed to the well-being of her students, she now has a strong interest in finding ways for children to get enough exercise to be healthy. From her readings of medical, psychological, and educational literature about the critical role physical activity plays in children's healthy development, lisa became convinced that physical activity should not be just an after-school add-on but, instead, included in the daily schedule of school. She thus decided to devote some time to figuring out how to incorporate into her pre-K classroom the sixty minutes a day of physical activity recommended to schools by medical and other professional organizations.[8] In doing this lisa hoped as well to alter her own reluctance to engage in physical activity.

She began her inquiry with a lot of questions: What is actually meant by the recommendation of one hour a day of physical activity? What are the benefits of so much physical activity? What are the areas inside and outside the school that can be used for physical activity by young children? What games and organized physical activities are appropriate for young children? What equipment/materials are needed for them? How could she connect young children's need for physical activity to her own life, where it had, thus far, held a very different value?

THE PROBLEM

Like many schools in urban areas, lisa's is housed in cramped quarters. It occupies the fourth floor—eighty-four steps up—of an old building that has been undergoing repairs for several years. Although the school has a small, attached play area that is equipped for young children, at the time of her study it was underneath scaffolding due to a renovation and thus was not usable. The only space available for outdoor play was a big cement schoolyard with lines painted on it, which children use for hopscotch, basketball, and other group games.

Although many public playgrounds are within a short walking distance, the time available to get to them and back is limited. The school's schedule is organized so that lisa's class has only about thirty minutes of outdoor time each day. Because it takes about ten minutes to walk back and forth from the school to the nearest playground, only about ten minutes is left for actual play. lisa questioned whether or not it was worth it to take this trip for such a short amount of time. Even when, on occasion, a full hour could be set aside for outside time, which was sufficient to go to a playground or on a neighborhood walk, rain or inclement weather often made it impossible for the class to leave the school.

In addition to these constraints, lisa had yet another concern: when the children actually got to a playground, not everyone got involved in physical activity. While some children would slide down the poles or the slide and others would run or play games of tag, there would always be some who would prefer to huddle together making up imaginative games that precluded any physical activity. What, lisa wondered, should she do about these children? Should she insist they use the time for physical activity?

To answer these questions lisa made a conscious effort to observe and document the different physical activities—both structured and unstructured—that took place in her classroom and in outside play spaces. She was curious to find out what opportunities for movement occurred naturally throughout the school day and how she could increase the impact of these and other physical activities. As she kept notes and took photographs of her classroom's daily happenings, new insights emerged about her teaching. She also gained a different perspective on her personal inclinations toward exercise and physical activity.

INSIGHT NO. 1: A SCHOOL DAY ORGANIZED TO PROVIDE ACTIVE LEARNING EXPERIENCES OFFERS NUMEROUS OPPORTUNITIES FOR CHILDREN'S BODIES AND MINDS TO ENGAGE IN LEARNING

lisa began her study of physical activity worrying that she would be unable to provide one hour of physical activity for her students each day so that they could obtain and sustain optimal physical health. But as she made observations over time, she realized that, throughout the school day, natural movement was supported and encouraged in many ways both inside and outside her classroom.

Outdoor Physical Activities

Looking first at the thirty minutes of her class's daily outside time revealed to lisa that there were in fact many potential options for activity. Although the school yard was devoid of equipment, lisa realized that she could easily facilitate and supply the fun. A few props could prompt the children to invent their own games. For example, one day two orange traffic cones were found in the school yard and used by Efram and Brandon to develop a game. lisa watched them carry the cones and place them on the blacktop's painted lines, tilting them first one way and then another. Later Lana, joining Efram, who had placed one cone on top of the other, climbed up to stand on the rim of the top cone. They were pretending they were on a sailboat's mast. Even such unintended play items inspired imagination and lots of fun.

On another day lisa brought out beanbags and a low cardboard box, making certain that every child had one beanbag to throw. When she offered to use these to play catch with the children, eager participants quickly surrounded her. Other children played on their own, throwing their bags through the basketball hoop. Did it matter that they didn't "get it in"? Not to them, as the fun seemed to be in the trying. Later another group of children was attracted to the low cardboard box that lisa brought out. Andrew walked up to the box and dropped his beanbag in it. A new game was created when lisa suggested he try throwing the beanbag from a longer distance. Balls and scoops made from cleaned plastic jugs with the bottoms cut off were also a hit with the children. Playing together and alone, they tossed the balls to each other back and forth, trying to catch them in the scoops.

lisa observed that if she interacted, even without props, with children who were reluctant to engage in physical activity, she could entice them to get involved. An example: Cailyn insisted one chilly morning that she was too cold to move. No amount of lisa's talking to her could convince Cailyn that moving her body would help her warm up. But when lisa made up a walking game in which they walked together when lisa said "go" and stopped together when lisa said "stop," Cailyn began to move to the rhythm of the words. "Go, go, go, go, go, go, stop." Each time lisa said these words, she said them faster. By the time the two reached the other side of the school yard, several other players had joined in. Cailyn soon assumed the role of prompter, taking full control of the game.

On the days when lisa's class had more time to be outside, she ventured with the children to neighboring playgrounds. When they were in these spaces, lisa observed, more of them actively engaged in play—a testimony to the power of a well-planned environment. The class's favorite playground was at a neighboring school. Designed by the school's students and teachers, it had swings, climbing walls, pull/chin-up bars, slides, a circular ladder, and a metal contraption with seats suspended in the air. Here children could walk, bounce, sway, or just sit. They really enjoyed taking turns on the swings, helping each other on and off, and pushing each other higher and higher. lisa helped facilitate their interactions and taught them how to "pump" with their legs.

Through observations of activities like these, lisa's investigation was revealing many ways that her students were active outdoors.

Physical Activity in the Classroom

The biggest revelation lisa had as a result of her observations was how much physical activity is actually involved in the learning experiences she provides *inside* her classroom. In addition to the formal time set aside for movement activities (a music and movement teacher visits the class once a week), a typical day in her classroom is filled with opportunities for physical activity. It looks something like the following:

Starting the Day   Each morning at the start of the school day, the children gather together in the school's play yard. They walk up the six flights of stairs to their classroom while lisa leads them in a song that tells them what to do, where to be, and how to be safe. To the tune of "The Farmer in the Dell," the children sing: "We're walking up the stairs. We're walking up the stairs. Ssh. Ssh. Sshsshsshssh. We're walking up the stairs." The verses continue with "We're holding onto the railing" and "We're standing next to our partner." This song helps the children keep the pace for walking up the stairs. At the third floor the class stops and does breathing exercises, then continues on up to their classroom.

Class Meetings   Once in the classroom, the children move about the room doing jobs like feeding the classroom animals and watering the plants. They gather together for a class meeting, which regularly includes a movement activity like stretching or doing finger plays or singing other songs that involve movement. They start slowly with a finger play such as "Tommy Thumb." This draws the children's attention to the smallest parts of their bodies and serves as a warm-up for further gross motor activity. The next song, "Open, Shut Them" adds to the momentum, stretching arms and legs, and adding hilarity as the children "do not let them in." The children put imaginary glue on their feet before standing up and moving to an expanded version of "Head, Shoulders, Knees, and Toes." After the first time this familiar song is sung, the children touch their heads but do not say the word. The next time, they touch their heads and shoulders but do not name either. By the time the song is finished, the children have done five sets of calisthenics. Now thoroughly warmed up, they are ready to move to the next song, one that encourages the children's verbal as well as physical participation, such as "Shake Your Sillies Out" or another favorite, "See How I'm Jumping." These songs incorporate gross motor activity with a period in each that brings the body back to a calm place to start again. For example, in "See How I'm Jumping" the children jump like frogs, stand still, jump again, and then huddle on the floor before standing partially up to use their arms to evoke images of thunder and lightning. At the end of the song ("They all stand up") the children may begin the song again or, if lisa thinks they have lost interest or simply had enough, she says, "They all sit down." And they willingly do so to catch their breath!

Music and Movement Time   Several times during the week, lisa leads the children in formal movement activities. On rainy days she becomes a DJ, beginning the movement time with slow warm-ups and continuing with music that previously has been introduced. Once a week there is an additional movement activity based on the favorite music of a rotating selection of children. Choices range from "I Wanna Be Sedated" by the Ramones, "Step in Time" from the musical *Mary Poppins*, "Thriller" by Michael Jackson, as well as assorted traditional children's music. As the children make a human train to travel from the meeting area to the block area (their dance space), the child who brought in the music leads the way. Everyone sings "My Body Makes Music" to keep minds and bodies busy along the way. Then they listen to the new music and dance in different ways.

When a child is reluctant to dance, lisa steps in to entice her. One day lisa noticed two girls, Aisha and Tamika, refusing to dance with anyone, no matter the music or the prompting. At first she wondered if the free dance was too overwhelmingly free for these typically quiet, reserved children.

However, she observed that the girls began to participate when someone brought in a children's song that directed more of the actions. After that, lisa made a conscious effort to mix different types of music into the movement time to open up a way for more children to participate.

Work Time   At Work Time children are given the opportunity to select activities in different areas of the room. Typically the areas that are "open" to the children are Pretend, Play dough, Sewing, Blocks, Sand, Painting, Animal Study, Writing, and Library. In each of these areas the children are active. At no time are they asked to sit or be still. They stand while painting at the table; in the play dough area they stand or sit, pounding, pressing, and rolling with their hands and arms. The pretend area is set up with big blocks and a wooden box, the top of which the children use as an imaginary stage, car, or bed. The wooden blocks, so heavy they need to be carried with two hands, get transformed through the children's activities into a bed, a car, or a barrier to the outside. At the sand table the children stand reaching across the sand, filling and pouring sand out of different size containers. In the writing area children busily bring their chosen materials—such as staplers, Scotch tape, scissors, stickers, as well as paper and crayons—to the writing table to use. In the library children read books, practice writing numbers on the green board, or draw their own pictures, reaching high on the hanging chart paper to draw and write with magic markers.

Transitioning from One Activity to Another   At the end of Work Time the children clean up the area they were working in. Materials are put away, tables are washed, and chairs are pushed under tables. They all meet back in the meeting area for a book or a share before lunch.

To help everyone get to their activities during Work Time, one child has the job of choosing how the other children will move to their chosen activities. This "Movement Helper" selects a movement that all the other children will use. The children use a variety of movements, such as galloping, sashaying, or tiptoeing. Some invent complex moves, such as putting hands and feet on the floor, and then twirling their bodies. The children seem to enjoy the fun of inventing new things to do.

Even the transition to lunch involves physical activity. Sometimes lisa asks each child to do an umbrella walk (hands on their heads, legs apart making big strides as they turn in slow circles) on their way to the table where the food is served. At other times she has the children do different movements like "Jump three times." A favorite variation replaces the direction with "Do whatever you want." This leads to all kinds of movements, which, lisa notices, are performed differently by each child:

> It is here that I notice the diverse dance movements that the children employ to express themselves. Brandon hops up when his name is called and immediately dives to the floor. He spins around on one hand, gracefully moving back and forth, his long hair flopping in its ponytail with his body movements. His form of break dancing looks as if it was learned through imitation. Alexa chooses to move slowly across the rug, arms raised above her head. Her body is as graceful as her four-year-old concentration will allow.

Lunch, Rest, and Other Events   The rest of the day contains continued opportunities for movement and action. At lunchtime, the children carry their lunch trays to their tables, serve themselves, and clean up. After that, a whirlwind of activity takes place. To prepare for rest time, each child gets a mat from a stack on the floor, places it in his/her own special spot, covers it with a sheet and blanket, and lies down for a bit.

After the children get up from their naps, they put away their rest things and then select, from easily accessible shelves, the materials they want to use. These have been put there to encourage the development of fine motor skills and/or to increase language development. Legos, puzzles, and buttons and strings are carried in big plastic bins to tables where groups of children can work on them together. Sometimes the floor is used to put together a big dinosaur or alphabet puzzle. At all times the children are moving to get, replace, or engage in activities.

Transitioning Home   When it is time to go home, the children put the materials back in their bins and then place the bins back on the shelves. After listening to and discussing one final book, the children select a book to take home, bring their book bags and coats from their cubbies to their tables, pack the book bags, and put on their coats.

At the end of the day, the class descends the stairs, all six flights, singing songs such as "Willoughby Wallaby" or "Today Is Monday" or "The Ants Go Marching In." Singing these songs requires concentration that helps the children pace their steps.

All in all, the children experience a very active, moving-about day. Reflecting on these images of what the class day looks like, lisa realized how much movement and action actually takes place: "Every day the children in my pre-K class are using their bodies to actively engage in learning to work with materials, their ideas, and each other—in other words, what I believe *is* the work of a pre-kindergartener."

INSIGHT NO. 2: A TEACHER'S KNOWLEDGE OF CHILDREN'S DEVELOPMENTAL NEEDS CAN ENHANCE PHYSICAL ACTIVITY FOR YOUNG CHILDREN IN SCHOOL

Young children are naturally energetic. They need to physically interact with the concepts and skills that they are learning. As they develop cognitively, they are also learning to control their bodies and energies within the constraints of the classroom.

From her years of experience working with young children, lisa understands these developmental needs. She understands how a child feels when a rainy day means there will be no outside play, how difficult it can be for a child to concentrate on what someone else is saying if he or she needs to consciously (or unconsciously) fight the impulse to move. It is because of this understanding that lisa has designed her classroom environment and the routines described earlier to invite children's continual movement:

> I begin by sculpting the classroom environment. There is room to walk to every area in the classroom. This space is typically large enough for two children to pass each other without touching. Tables, shelves, and the meeting area rug are placed maze-like to allow for slower movement that considers space and destination. A toddler's wooden bridge is used in place of one of these walkways as an extra activity for those who choose it. The largest open spaces are in the block area and in the meeting area. The block area is used not only for block building but for whole-group dancing. The meeting area is the heart of our classroom. We meet and move here, look at books, examine the nature table, and, when we are all together, sit quietly, thinking and sharing ideas.

Another example of how lisa has structured the physical design of her class to incorporate her understanding of children's natural energy is what she has done with the area where children enter and leave the classroom. Two rows of black footprints are painted on the floor, two sets across, so children easily know where to line up individually or with a partner as they prepare to leave the room. The design of this space enables them to engage each other and their bodies in different ways while heeding the requirement that their feet must not leave the footprints. Children turn, feet still firmly on the prints, to talk to the child behind them. Spontaneous trains are formed when the participants place their hands on the shoulders of the children in front of them and gently sway to music that is being played. Sometimes children will take advantage of the space and jump from one set of footprints to the empty set ahead of them. In these ways, the children are learning to stand, to wait, and to move with a twist of exuberance that is so characteristic of young children.

REFLECTIONS ON LEARNING IN ACTIVE WAYS

Through her investigation of how to incorporate more physical activity into her classroom, lisa's awareness of the importance of physical activity was not only validated—it was heightened. More strongly than ever she became convinced that children learn by doing; that activity is their natural way of learning; that a lack of opportunity for movement is detrimental to their development because, in order to learn, young children need to move.

Another lesson that lisa took away from her investigation is that a teacher's engagement with children in physical activity can benefit the teacher as well as the child. By playing and moving about with the children, lisa enriched her relationships with them. Engaging with them in these ways gave her new perspectives and understanding about them. But her physical engagement with the children was beneficial to her own self as well. It brought a new vitality to her mind, body, and spirit:

> I observed in myself, when I played with the children, that I felt better physically and more energetic throughout the day. This activity rekindled memories of my childhood. I remembered how much I liked to run, climb, throw, and catch in playful, noncompetitive games. I remembered how important the lack of competition was to me, as was the freedom to move.
>
> Most important, I felt more connected to the children. This was true especially of the child who didn't seem to want to play with the other children and seemed just to want to talk to the teacher. That desire to talk to the teacher, to be seen or noticed, was a strong one in

my childhood. When Brandon was in the school yard he consistently stood talking to a teacher. Earlier I would try and engage Brandon in play with other children but he would always gravitate back to me, sidling up with something he wanted to say. How different it felt to play with scoops and balls or toss the beanbag back and forth with Brandon. It seemed like a different kind of communication, one that he never tired of as long as the ball or beanbag was in play.

Although most of what lisa read about how to enhance children's physical activity advocated organized classes as the primary way for children to acquire motor, stability, and manipulative skills,[9] her investigation into how a teacher can support physical activity in the classroom led her to form a different opinion. From her study she concluded that prescribed programs and curricula are not the only ways to support physical activity. Rather, from her experiences she came to understand that knowledgeable and engaged teachers can get children moving by setting up a classroom and routines that have many opportunities for activity, by making available developmentally appropriate equipment and materials, and by engaging with the children in the use of these materials.

LOOKING AHEAD TO IMPROVED TEACHING

As a result of her study, lisa made several goals for herself for her future years of teaching in relation to physical activity. One was to share more with families about the importance of physical activity in their children's lives. In her narrative reports about each child, which she writes twice a year and sends home to each family, she vowed to include a section on "the physical child." In it she would include her documentation of their experiences and growth in academic and social/emotional arenas. "This will help to make active learning more visible in the prekindergarten day. I want families to know that the development of healthy, physically active habits is implicit in my class."

lisa also came away from her study convinced that teachers in schools, regardless of how many resources are available to them or how test-driven their school curricula are, need to know that they (the teachers) are a critical resource for their students' lifelong habits and interests in physical activity; that by supporting physical activity throughout the day, teachers are working *with* and *for* children. The physical activity does not have to be fancy. It can involve simply enhancing, in creative and meaningful ways, children's movements that occur naturally throughout the school day. This includes making available age-appropriate equipment that builds on children's natural impetus to play.

One other insight that lisa took from her study was how important it is for policy makers to understand the urgency of the fact that our nation is increasingly producing new generations of inactive, overweight, play-inhibited children. Educators need to be supported to combat this trend and reverse it. lisa is convinced that ". . . support will be given only when policy makers begin to see the connection between children's need for physical activity and real educational [as well as personal] success."

As teachers like lisa explore such issues related to their practice, they make the "inside of teaching" visible to others—the problems, the strengths, and the challenges. In this way, teacher research can inform teachers' practice, families' understanding, and, it is hoped, the making of systemic policy.

Ideas from Inside lisa's Classroom

♦ A teacher's engagement with children in physical activity can benefit the teacher as well as the child. The interaction can enrich the child-teacher relationship, giving the teacher an added window of understanding about the child.

♦ Teachers can infuse physical activity into daily classroom life by taking advantage of natural movement opportunities in creative and imaginative ways.

♦ To enrich and support children's physical activity throughout the school day, teachers can set up the classroom with opportunities for activity, create routines that include times for movement, make available developmentally appropriate equipment and materials, and engage with the children in the use of these materials.

CHAPTER 15

What Can a Teacher Do to Improve the Climate for Learning in a School?: Laurie Jagoda

From the moment you enter a school, you can feel whether or not it has a positive climate. Is there a sense of calmness and order? Is there an excitement for learning that permeates the air? Are there school symbols, traditions, and celebrations of achievement visible as you walk down the hallways? Is there a collegial, enthusiastic spirit among teachers? Moreover, is there a feeling of community, where students and teachers are motivated to work hard because they are committed to the school's success?

Laurie Jagoda was interested in helping her school improve its learning climate. Over her six years of experience teaching in urban schools, she came to see that many schools fail to exploit the direct link between the quality of a school's climate and its educational outcomes.[10] Concerns such as preparing students for standardized tests and aligning curriculum with state standards have in many schools taken precedence over developing a positive school culture. At the time of her inquiry, Laurie had been teaching middle school for two years at the Citizens of the Future

Charter School.[11] She wanted to explore how, in her position as a teacher, she could spearhead initiatives that would improve her school's climate for learning.

WHY SCHOOL CULTURE?

Through reading the extensive literature on the topic, Laurie learned that a positive school culture begins with a shared vision and that, in the best of circumstances, a school's vision is the result of an intensive process of consensus building by its different stakeholders.[12] This process of bringing in the different constituent groups is especially vital for newly created schools such as Laurie's, which are founded on the idealistic principles of the individuals who pioneered them.[13] Ideally, teachers and administrators work together to shape their school's direction during its initial years. Decisions such as curriculum selection, pedagogical methods, discipline policies, and uniform codes are chosen based on a core ideology.

GETTING STARTED

Laurie began her investigation by visiting schools with similar populations to her own that have been recognized for their positive cultures. Her purpose was to take what she learned from these places to craft improvement initiatives in her situation. As she set out to gather examples of what each school did to build and maintain a positive climate, she focused on how they developed a collective vision, supported the school's rituals and ceremonies, included student voices in the work of the school, and provided teachers with support. Simultaneously, in her own school, she formed a School Culture Committee with seven colleagues, with the intention of launching initiatives that would put into practice some of what she was learning.

CHARACTERISTICS OF POSITIVE SCHOOL CULTURES

From her visits to other schools, Laurie discovered that the educational vision of each school was apparent in every aspect of daily life—through the visual symbols displayed throughout the school, the language shared among community members, and the teaching practices found in the classrooms. In all of the schools, students were encouraged to play an active role—either through student councils, peer juries, or honor committees. Each school also had schoolwide celebrations, such as awards assemblies or cultural events. Teacher support was also evident in all of the settings: the leaders incorporated collaborative planning, professional development, and teacher observations into the schools' weekly schedules.

IMPLEMENTING SCHOOLWIDE INITIATIVES

The School Culture Committee that Laurie launched included her, Mr. O'Brien (the dean of students), and six teachers who had previously served on a short-lived "school improvement team." At their first meeting, Laurie explained her understanding of the definition of school culture and then led the group in a discussion about some of the positive and negative qualities of the school. The strengths of the school noted by the group included a dynamic staff, strong student-teacher relationships, and the fact that teachers were involved in curriculum development. Areas identified as in need of improvement included the ways that preparation for high-stakes standardized tests dominated everyone's teaching practices, a lack of communication among the faculty, and insufficient feedback and professional development to enhance the teachers' learning.

Laurie shared with the group some of what she had learned from her readings about the importance of developing a "collective" vision. After a lengthy brainstorming session and several rough drafts, the committee crafted a vision statement of their own:

Citizens of the Future Charter School will develop within their students a positive attitude toward education so that they will become articulate, confident, lifelong learners. The students will become socially conscious individuals who embody the character traits of respect and integrity. They will graduate from college and become successful in any field that they pursue, inspiring change for future generations.

As a result of this meeting, Laurie developed an understanding of the delicate balance that needs to maintained to be both a teacher and a leader in her community: "I am relieved that teachers were receptive to my ideas and genuinely seemed interested in my research. I was apprehensive at first, because I am their colleague, not their administrator, and I did not want to be perceived as authoritative or pompous . . . but now I feel confident that they support my efforts to bring much-needed changes to the school."

At a subsequent School Culture Committee meeting, members brainstormed the ways a common vision could be infused into school life. Focusing on rituals and ceremonies, support for teachers, and eliciting student voices, the group created a large web to visually demonstrate how these components are interconnected and how each one cannot thrive without the others. Committee members then set about mapping out an action plan for how they would accomplish their stated goals.

The following week, the group presented their ideas to the entire school staff. After discussing and revising the proposed vision statement and sharing the web as well as the action plan, each teacher committed to take on a task. Laurie was anxious about this meeting, wondering how teachers would react to having additional responsibilities added to their already-full plates. "Would they take this seriously?" she wondered. " My dean and I alone cannot make all teachers be on board with these initiatives. Was I too presumptuous in thinking all teachers would follow through with their task?" Her fears, however, were not warranted, as will be demonstrated in the description of the following events.

Involving Students

To support their goal of enhancing student voice, the School Culture Committee brought the idea of creating a student government to the student body, launching an election process for the coming year. It was kicked off by an energetic lunchtime speech from the dean of students, followed with the distribution of nomination ballots by the committee. The following weeks were filled with a flurry of election activities: candidate speeches, debates, and a formal voting process.

The process of forming a student council generated unprecedented interest and excitement across the school. A surge of positive energy spread throughout the building. Laurie, as well as the other teachers, was amazed at how passionately the students were involved. As one teacher noted, "It was incredibly clear that all of the students were engaged in a real way—from those who do not typically care much about school to the top achievers . . . . You don't really see that here very often." Laurie was particularly pleased about this because inspiring students, especially middle schoolers, to feel passionate about anything is not an easy feat. Her excitement about the possibilities was reflected in the following entry she made in her journal: "Today, during the seventh grade debates, I looked around the room and saw an audience that was shockingly quiet and attentive. I do not think I have ever seen the students with such a focused stare on the speaker, surely not when I am teaching in my classroom."

Fueled by the opportunity to have a voice, the students took their elections seriously, evaluating the candidates on the merits of their proposals rather than on whether or not they were "popular." The seventh grade president confirmed this when he remarked, "I know students took it seriously because they voted for me and I was not as popular as my opponent."

A new sense of possibility among the students was ignited by the election-week activities. Among comments that Laurie overheard was the following by a student who credited the elections with giving "us the feeling that choice mattered; we felt powerful. It made students think that they can change things." A sense of responsibility among the students also seemed to be born: the newly elected student council officers consciously saw themselves as role models for others and promised to bring their ideas for school improvement—from better school lunch menus and schoolwide activities to a say in the curriculum chosen for them—to the administration. Noting how the elections "gave students the opportunity to own something in the building," the dean of students commented that "it wasn't just another lesson or assignment that was handed down—this was something organically drawn out of them."

The election experience also helped build community within the school. Both teachers and students noted how everyone came together during this time. Candidates called on their peers to become campaign managers; students got involved in designing and hanging up posters throughout the school; teachers helped with speechwriting; and even parents became involved by helping to design campaign ads. Laurie was delighted to see former "enemies helping each other put up posters, campaign managers giving up their recess to help their candidates with their speeches, and teachers rallying together to help out in any way."

Teachers were affected by the experience as well, particularly in the ways that their relationships with students were strengthened. Seventh grade English language arts teacher Ms. Watson said, "Some of the most meaningful moments I have had working at this school happened when I sat down with another teacher to help students write their speeches. We really felt like we were seeing kids in a different light." The high quality of students' speeches, their cordial behavior, and the serious tone the students exhibited during the elections gave many teachers an image of the academic rigor that could be possible in their classrooms.

Students' expectations for success were also heightened as a result of the election experiences. Students became conscious of how their actions could help everyone hold higher expectations for their behavior. This awareness is evident in the comments of the ninth grader who said, "Now that I am vice president, teachers expect me to show other kids what to do. . . . I have to be on my best behavior because if they see that I am bad, then students will think they can be bad . . . and if the VP is doing it, then why not?"

Clearly, creating a student government impacted the school's culture in a positive way. It heightened students' interest and excitement, encouraged their autonomy and responsibility, and raised everyone's overall expectations.

Schoolwide Celebrations

Schoolwide celebrations and rituals help to create a positive school climate. The inauguration ceremony that the School Culture Committee held for the newly elected student council was a great beginning event. Teachers got involved by overseeing committees that took responsibility for providing food, decorations, invitations, and student performances. Laurie was thrilled by their actions. It was exactly what she had hoped for. "I can't remember a time when teachers at Citizens of the Future Charter School were this energized or excited," she said. "Teachers were throwing out ideas right and left and taking on responsibilities voluntarily." This involvement was creating a new atmosphere at the school. As one teacher noted, "The sense of community at this moment was overwhelming."

Other schoolwide events soon followed the inauguration ceremony. Most notable was a celebration of Barack Obama's election, planned by the School Culture Committee in recognition of his historic election to the presidency and the special significance of the event for the school's predominantly African American community. Laurie explained, "His achievements sent the message to all of us that what may seem unimaginable is now possible; that no dream is too far-fetched. We wanted the students to remember the magnitude of this moment by sharing it with their school community."

Many teachers used this celebration, along with subsequent school events, as an opportunity to enrich their curricula. For example, during the week prior to the event, fifth grade social studies teacher Ms. Jones connected President Obama's story to her class's study of U.S. history. As part of the study she had her students construct a time line of pivotal moments in black history. Additionally, she asked them to reflect on what being an American meant to them. These were videotaped and shown at the Obama celebration. She also directed them in a performance of President Obama's "Yes We Can" speech. Creating the set design was the art teacher, who decorated the gymnasium with student paintings depicting students' visions of a changing world. This event "was the first time the entire school convened to showcase their creativity and voices," one of the teachers commented. "Students engaged in teamwork, cooperative learning, and collective efforts toward a common goal . . . . The celebration gave us an opportunity to utilize the creativity and passion of the students and the vast resources of the school."

In addition to these two major ceremonies, the School Culture Committee initiated still other projects. Included were a monthly assembly, the purpose of which was to recognize students' and teachers' accomplishments, and a "student of the month" bulletin board set up in the cafeteria to acknowledge those who made outstanding achievements. School rituals and ceremonies such as these "summon[ed] spirit by reinvigorating cultural cohesion and focus."[14]

Teachers Support Teachers

Laurie's investigation of how to improve school climate revealed the need for a system of support for the teachers in her school: veteran teachers expressed their need for meaningful professional development and novice teachers desperately wanted help in dealing with the challenges of classroom management. All of the teachers, whether experienced or novice, wanted time to get together to discuss and plan their work. "We need time to identify, in a more comprehensive way, what exactly the kids need to know, how we can assess it, and how we can ensure that the instruction really tailors to those needs," noted one veteran teacher.

When Laurie brought these concerns to the School Culture Committee, the group decided that two areas—teacher mentoring for novice teachers and collaborative planning time—were the most pressing. They scheduled a meeting with the school's administrative team to present a proposal for concrete action. Although Laurie felt anxious about bringing these issues to the administration, she bolstered her resolve by reminding herself of what she had learned from her visits to other successful schools and what she had read in the school reform literature about how "collegial support and interaction enable individual teachers to revise their classroom practice and make breakthroughs in their own learning . . . It is these knowledge-sharing strategies that contribute most to teacher success."[15]

Strengthened by all she had seen and read, Laurie proposed—when the meeting with the administration actually happened—that the school establish a mentoring program for novice teachers and create a peer-observation protocol. To her surprise, the principal agreed to both. She was also able to negotiate a reorganization of the school schedule to create a common planning time for teachers in each grade. The only catch was that all of this change work was left to her and the other teachers to make happen. While feeling defeated about this at first, the teachers quickly realized that they had indeed accomplished a victory; they came to understand that the only way change was going to happen was for them to stop waiting for their school leaders to take action and instead take responsibility for making change into their own hands.

So Laurie and her colleagues created a peer-observation form that they now use with each other twice a month. Biweekly team meetings have also been arranged so that teachers can regularly get together to discuss issues pertaining to their students and the curriculum. In addition, a few veteran teachers have volunteered to mentor some of the novice teachers.

SHARING THE LEARNING

Through her efforts, Laurie has learned much about what constitutes a positive culture in a school. She has come to understand the interrelationship between school climate and efforts to make change, noting how "beliefs and actions of faculty and students, the ways in which special moments are celebrated, and how teachers are supported to be successful in their practice" all need to be in sync in order for a school to achieve its desired goals. Many teachers are not aware of all of these aspects and complexities of change. While they may see that their school culture is in need of strengthening, they have little idea about how to change it or where to begin. Laurie hopes that sharing the work she and her colleagues have done will help others who may be interested in launching their own school improvement initiatives.

Ideas from Inside Laurie's Classroom

◆ Teachers can be leaders in organizing students and teachers to engage in school change initiatives.

◆ Key aspects to building a positive school culture are: developing a collective vision; creating school rituals, traditions, and ceremonies; including student voice in the governance of the school; and providing support for teachers to work together.

◆ Visiting schools to observe innovations in settings similar to your own school can be informative and inspiring. The visit can also introduce you to a professional contact who can be a valuable resource.

◆ Although spearheading change initiatives can be time- and energy- intensive, it can also be invigorating and lead to professional growth.

Inquiry and Powerful Urban Teaching

The stories presented in this book reveal how teachers' inquiries into their work help them to learn about and contribute to the understanding of teaching and learning. The accounts shed light on four important aspects of effective urban teaching:

- Using the richness of students' and families' cultural backgrounds as a resource for teaching and learning;

- Creating strong home/school partnerships with families and communities across diverse languages and cultures;

- Differentiating instruction to ensure that every child is supported to learn at the best of his/her abilities;

- Negotiating the constraints of mandated practices and policies in schools to ensure that children are taught in the ways that they learn.

CULTURALLY RESPONSIVE TEACHING

The first section, which described the work of Beatrice Tinio, Joleen Hanlon, Adesina Abani, and Mary Williams, focused on investigations into how to teach in culturally responsive ways. While the individuals whose stories we have recounted all come from different backgrounds, they share the view that in order for teachers to be effective supporters of children's learning, especially of those from diverse cultural and linguistic backgrounds, they must seek to understand their students and then use this understanding as a resource in their teaching. Their accounts reveal the challenges involved in helping children make connections between their experiences in school and in their home lives. They offer us images of successful ways to bring the perspectives of diverse languages, cultures, races, and religions into the classroom and to use these to enrich our teaching.

STRONG HOME/SCHOOL PARTNERSHIPS

The power and potential of school/family partnerships to bridge differences across cultures, languages, and socioeconomic backgrounds is richly exemplified in the stories of Evelyn Chang, Joan O'Brien, Kanene Holder, Rory Scott, and Kisha Pressley. Collectively, their investigations demonstrate the importance of including families in school life in order to support students' educational needs. Such efforts deepen educators' understanding of the strengths and challenges of the communities represented in their schools and help them to value and use families as resources for students' learning. The vivid accounts of the work of the group of educators featured in this section also highlight how school/family partnerships help families better understand the approaches to learning that take place in the school so that the families can be better equipped to support their children's learning at home. These stories remind us how sharing among all the stakeholders in a school can contribute to the creation of a learning community that enhances the growth and development of all.

DIFFERENTIATING TEACHING
TO ENSURE OPTIMAL LEARNING

In the third section of this volume we focused on what Neurys Bonilla, Carol Castillo, and Travis Sloane learned about the power of customizing teaching to support each child's learning. Their stories demonstrate how, whether one is working with children in a dual-language or multiage classroom or with children who are identified as having special needs, careful documentation of how students progress and carry out their learning is essential to good teaching. The combined practices of close observation of what children know and do, thoughtful reflection about this evidence, and careful attention to the selection of teaching strategies help teachers build on children's strengths, address their challenges, and support them to become powerful learners.

NEGOTIATING THE CONSTRAINTS
OF URBAN TEACHING

In our final section we described teachers' efforts to negotiate curriculum and testing mandates in order to ensure their students' optimal learning. Hazel Veras-Gomez examined how to infuse developmentally appropriate learning activities into her kindergarten's test-driven curriculum. Prekindergarten teacher lisa schaffner explored how to provide her class with daily physical activity in the midst of the academic pressures influenced by high-stakes accountability policies. Laurie Jagoda inquired about how to develop a professional school culture in the standards-dominated atmosphere of her middle school. Each of these stories reveal the possibilities of how teachers can assume leadership and take charge of their professional lives.

TEACHER EMPOWERMENT

The accounts presented here are but a few of many from the creative teachers with whom we have had the privilege to learn over the past years. While the investigations we have shared here are now completed, many of the featured teacher-researchers continue to question, inquire, develop new understanding, collaborate, and share their work. The process of engaging in their own inquiries has seemed to ignite a "flow" (a term first coined by psychologist Mihaly Csikszentmihalyi[1] to represent the ultimate in positive, focused energy and motivation toward a task at hand) that drives them to keep learning, sharing, collaborating, and taking on new challenges in their professional lives. Some of the teacher-researchers have become leaders in their schools, using their knowledge to provide professional development to colleagues, to create their own study groups, and to launch their own educational organizations. Others have shared their research through different genres (a one-woman show, a journal article, a poetry slam) that they have presented publicly. Still others have even sought further graduate study. Their ongoing process of learning is captured well by the comment of our teacher colleague Mercedes Orozco: "Once begun, the research process never ends. It continues in our classrooms today."[2]

TEACHER PROFESSIONALISM

While their inquiries about teaching have been important to the lives of the teachers who are featured here, teacher research, from a policy perspective, has relevance to the field of education as a whole. All across the globe, educational issues are at center stage as nations and policy makers search for ways to improve schooling and student achievement. In the United States this quest is seen as being linked to the viability of our country's economy and the very survival of our democracy. Yet our efforts toward improvement that politically have gained traction are dramatically different than those that are used in the nations identified as having the highest-achieving students (Finland, Singapore, and Canada). Unlike those educationally successful countries, which have adopted a capacity-building approach to educational improvement, the United States has focused much of its improvement efforts on mandates about what and how to teach that are enforced by frequent high-stakes tests, and followed by punishments for students, teachers, and schools whose performance do not meet required expectations.

In contrast, the globe's highest-achieving countries invest in supports for their teachers. They recruit highly qualified candidates, provide and pay for high-quality preparation, pay teachers decently once they enter the profession, assess their competencies through performance assessments (administered sparingly) that demonstrate how knowledge is applied to real-life problems, and attend to educators' learning—through shared planning, action research, lesson study, and observations in each other's classrooms—throughout the span of teachers' careers.[3]

As a result of such supports, these nations have produced a stable cadre of high-quality educators who are continually engaged in learning that both informs and is informed by their practice. Not coincidentally, much of what these educators do strongly resembles the careful inquiry about students and teaching represented in the teachers' stories here.

It is this kind of professionalism that we need more of to improve students' learning in the United States. When teachers are given opportunities to engage as questioners and reflectors about their work, they are able to construct new knowledge about teaching—to invent new solutions to nagging problems, identify new challenges that need to be addressed, and respond to the unique contexts and needs of the children and families of the communities in which they teach. Through ongoing investigation and reflection about practice, teachers can invent better ways to explain lessons, to entice reluctant learners, to bring unruly classes under control, and to ignite children's imaginations. As they exercise their intellect and judgment in these ways, teachers move away from being passive recipients

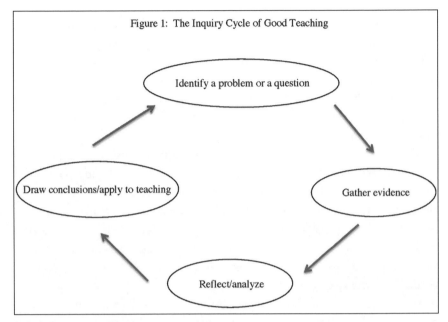

Figure 13.

of "teacher-proof" curricula and high-stakes tests that are imposed from above and instead become empowered to take charge of their teaching.[4] The professionalism that is the hallmark of high-achieving countries is indeed evident in this kind of work.

We believe the inquiry approach to teaching that is featured throughout the chapters of this book is an especially powerful tool for tackling the pressing issues, which often seem intractable, that are present disproportionately in high-poverty urban communities. The stories we have shared demonstrate how those on the inside of urban teaching are uniquely positioned to identify and find solutions to the many pressing problems that they face. The accounts offer insight into how to view difference as an asset, not a deficit, and how to be respectful of many perspectives.[5] They highlight the rich possibilities for learning in urban settings as they also model how educators can "take on new roles, hear diverse voices, develop . . . identity as urban educators, and engage in productive dialogue."[6]

UNPACKING THE COMPLEXITIES OF TEACHING

It is our hope that the ideas and practices we have presented can counter the images of test-driven teaching that are currently being promoted as reform in the United States. We offer them as an alternate vision—of teaching that is an iterative cycle of observation, documentation, and reflection to inform instruction and support students' learning. (See Figure 13).

More than a century ago John Dewey argued that the best theory is deeply practical and the best practice is deeply theoretical.[7] We believe that the images of teaching presented here exemplify Dewey's conceptualization. They reveal how teachers' practice-based research can create new knowledge about teaching and learning and contribute to efforts to provide the best possible education for *all* children, especially those in greatest need, in the schools of our diverse urban communities.

How This Book Was Constructed

The stories in this book were compiled from reports of teachers' research that were completed as the culminating project of a year-long course we teach in our teacher preparation programs at The City College of New York. For this project, teacher-learners are asked to propose, design, and carry out a study in their own classrooms or their schools. These studies primarily fall within Rock and Levin's definition of teacher action research as "systematic inquiry by teachers with the goal of improving their teaching practices."[1] Course participants are encouraged to select topics that are relevant and of interest to their lived experiences and then search for a deeper understanding of the issues and/or solutions to the proposed problems. Just as children make meaning of the world in social contexts and through experiences rather than via transmission modes of teaching,[2] the teachers who engage in our course's project discover how the theories and strategies they learn in their preparation program actually play out in their own classrooms. In doing this they experience the power of synthesizing and constructing their own understanding of teaching and learning in the specific contexts of urban life, with all of the complex issues and problems that affect how students learn and how teachers teach. Our earlier book, *The Power of Questions*,[3] describes in detail how we teach this course and offers step-by-step guidance to teachers on how they can conduct their own research projects.

When we first set out to write this book, we began by reviewing the research reports of the hundreds of teachers who have taken our course over the years. After identifying themes that ran across their work, we selected for this volume a diverse group of reports that we felt were especially compelling. We obtained approval from our college's internal review board and then invited the selected authors to participate in our project. Then we obtained their official consent and began crafting their stories into the chapters that appear here. When our first drafts were completed, we sent them to each of the teachers to review, asking them to respond to such questions as: Were there any inaccuracies in how we described your project? Were you surprised by the aspects of your study that we emphasized? Did we omit any information you felt should have been included? And how did it feel to read someone else's version of your story? Sometimes teachers reported that they did not see "inaccuracies" but felt our interpretation differed from theirs. We tried to be responsive to this feedback, often revising what we had written to better evoke the teachers' expressed meaning.

From their comments we also learned that some of the teachers felt there were advantages to someone else telling their story. Travis Sloane's comments are representative of this sentiment:

> I rather enjoyed reading someone else's version of my project. A different perspective, especially from someone who was not fully immersed in it, made apparent that what I had intended to research and record actually came across. Furthermore, a different perspective often highlights or underplays other aspects, identifying for me other

avenues that the research could have taken or where future research could go.

Many of the teachers, like Kanene Holder, expressed appreciation for being given the opportunity to share their learning: "I think being selected is . . . a great platform to spread a message about the results of building relationships with parents in the community. I hope the wider audience can learn from my process and be inspired to continue in their schools and communities."

We too hope that this book inspires and supports those who engage in the hard work of teaching. It is in this spirit that we share the teachers' stories presented here.

Eliciting Teacher-Researchers' Responses

QUESTIONS TO THE TEACHER-RESEARCHER

The following questions were sent to each author via e-mail along with a draft of the profile of their investigations. The author's response was then used to direct the subsequent revisions of the profile.

- How did it feel to read someone else's version of your research project?

- Were there any inaccuracies in how we described your research project?

- Did we emphasize any aspects of your study that surprised you in any way?

- Did we omit any information you felt should have been included? (Please be as specific as possible.)

- How do you feel about our perspective on your story?

- How do you feel about your project being selected to be a part of this book on the work of urban teacher-researchers?

- What would you like to say (words of advice, caution, etc.) to other teachers who might read about your work?

INTERVIEW GUIDE

These questions were posed at an in-person interview with the teacher-researcher after reading and responding to the "case" of their study:

Biographical information:

Your name:

Place of birth:

Education:

Family's education:

Where did you grow up?

Who raised you?

When did you take the research class at CCNY?

Where were you teaching at that time and has your career changed? Are you teaching in a new setting?

Comparing your education to your teaching experiences:

What was your (preschool, elementary school) like? How was your school similar or different from the school in which you currently teach (or taught in at the time of your research study)?

How is the community in which you grew up similar to or different from the community of the school in which you teach?

What are/were the challenges of teaching at your school? What are/were the advantages?

How did you know about the school's community before you started teaching in this school?

Can you provide any examples of how you draw on your knowledge of the community in your teaching?

Discussing your research:

What was your research project about?

How did you come to develop this question/area of interest?

Explain how/if your prior knowledge about the community in which you teach informed how you developed your research study.

Have you shared what you learned through your research project in any way? Shared information with colleagues? What has been the reaction?

What did you take away from your teacher research experience? What did you learn about your teaching?

What did you learn about yourself?

What specific pieces of data, aspects of the study, or kinds of learning have stayed with you?

Has the experience had an effect on your teaching? In what way(s)?

Are there any ways you have used aspects of the research process in your current teaching?

NOTES

INTRODUCTION:
QUESTIONING, SEARCHING, LEARNING FROM TEACHING

1. Paulo Freire, *Pedagogy of Freedom: Ethics, Democracy, and Civic Courage* (Lanham, MD: Rowman & Littlefield, 2000), 35.

2. Ranking America, "The U.S. Ranks 4th in Child Poverty," January 13, 2010, rankingamerica.wordpress.com/2010/01/13/the-u-s-ranks-2nd-in-child-poverty/.

3. Gloria Ladson-Billings, "From the Achievement Gap to the Education Debt: Understanding Achievement in U.S. Schools," *Educational Researcher* 35 (2006): 3–12.

4. Glenda Bissex and Richard H. Bullock, *Seeing for Ourselves: Case Study Research by Teachers of Writing* (Portsmouth, NH: Heinemann, 1987); D. Jean Clandinin and F. Michael Connelly, "Teachers' Professional Knowledge Landscapes: Secret, Sacred, and Cover Stories," in *Teachers' Professional Knowledge Landscapes*, ed. D. Jean Clandinin and F. Michael Connelly, 1–15 (New York: Teachers College Press, 1995); Marilyn Cochran-Smith and Susan L. Lytle, "Research on Teaching and Teacher Research: The Issues That Divide," *Educational Researcher* 19, no. 2 (1990): 2–11; Fred Erickson, "Qualitative Methods on Research on Teaching," in *Handbook of Research on Teaching*, 3rd ed., ed. Merlin C. Wittrock, 119–61 (New York: Macmillan, 1986); Susan Florio-Ruane and Martha Walsh, "The Teacher as Colleague in Classroom Research," in *Culture and the Bilingual Classroom: Studies in Classroom Ethnography*, ed. Henry T. Trueba, Grace Pung Guthrie, and Kathryn Hu-Pei Au, 87–101 (Rowley, MA: Newbury House, 1980); Susan L.

Lytle and Marilyn Cochran-Smith, "Teacher Researcher: Toward Clarifying the Concept," *National Writing Project Quarterly* 1, no. 3 (March 1989): 22–27; C. Gordon Wells, *The Meaning Makers: Children Learning Language and Using Language to Learn* (Portsmouth, NH: Heinemann, 1994).

5. Eudora Welty, *One Writer's Beginnings* (1983; Cambridge, MA: Harvard University Press, 2003).

6. Sara Lawrence-Lightfoot, *The Third Chapter: Passion, Risk and Adventure in the 25 Years After 50* (New York: Farrar, Straus and Giroux, 2010), 16.

7. Gloria Ladson-Billings, *The Dreamkeepers: Successful Teachers of African American Children* (San Francisco: Jossey-Bass, 1994).

SECTION 1: INSIDE CULTURALLY RESPONSIVE TEACHING

1. Adesina's name is a pseudonym.

2. Nicole Santa Cruz, "Minority Population Growing in the United States, Census Estimates Show," *Los Angeles Times*, June 10, 2010, articles.latimes.com/2010/jun/10/nation/la-na-census-20100611

3. Geneva Gay, "A Synthesis of Scholarship in Multicultural Education," North Central Regional Laboratory, 1994, www.ncrel.org/sdrs/areas/issues/educatrs/leadrshp/le0gay.htm; Sonia Nieto, *Affirming Diversity: The Sociopolitical Context of Multicultural Education*, 5th ed. (Amherst, MA: Pearson, 2008).

4. Gay, Lesbian, and Straight Education Network, "National School Climate Survey: Nearly 9 out of 10 LGBT Students Experience Harassment in School," September 14, 2010, www.glsen.org/cgi-bin/iowa/all/news/record/2624.html.

5. Jason Cianciotto and Sean Cahill, *Education Policy: Issues Affecting Lesbian, Gay, Bisexual, and Transgender Youth* (New York: National Gay and Lesbian Task Force Policy Institute, 2003), thetaskforce.org/reports_and_research/education_policy.

6. Massachusetts Department of Elementary and Secondary Education, "Youth Risk Behavior Survey," 2010, www.doe.mass.edu/cnp/hprograms/yrbs/; National Institute of Mental Health, "Suicide in the U.S.: Statistics and Prevention," 2010, www.nimh.nih.gov/health/publications/suicide-in-the-us-statistics-and-prevention/index.shtml.

7. R. Vigilante, "Winning in New York, New York: New York Board of Education Furor over Proposed Public School Curriculum Which Would

Teach Tolerance of Homosexuality and Safe Sex in AIDS Prevention," *National Review*, January 18, 1993.

8. Michael Wilhoite, *Daddy's Roommate* (New York: Alyson Wonderland, 1994).

9. Lesléa Newman and Diana Souza, *Heather Has Two Mommies* (New York: Alyson, 2009).

10. Pauline Lipman, "'Bringing Out the Best in Them': The Contribution of Culturally Relevant Teachers to Educational Reform," *Theory into Practice* 34, no. 3 (1995): 202–8.

11. Evelyn Jacob, "Reflective Practice and Anthropology in Culturally Diverse Classrooms," *Elementary School Journal* 95, no. 5 (1995): 451–63.

12. Bernard Waber, *Courage* (New York: Houghton Mifflin, 2002).

13. Jerry Spinelli, *Fourth Grade Rats* (New York: Scholastic, 1993).

14. Gloria Ladson-Billings, "Toward a Theory of Culturally Relevant Pedagogy," *American Educational Research Journal* 32, no. 3 (1995): 465–91.

15. Ann Cameron, *The Stories Julian Tells* (New York: Dell Yearling, 1981).

16. Tyrone C. Howard, "Culturally Relevant Pedagogy: Ingredients for Critical Teacher Reflection," *Theory into Practice* 42, no. 3 (2003): 195–202.

17. Lisa Campbell, *Sam Johnson and the Blue Ribbon Quilt* (New York: Mulberry Books, 1992).

18. R. Powell, "Then the Beauty Emerges: A Longitudinal Case Study of Culturally Relevant Teaching," *Teaching and Teacher Education* 13, no. 5 (1997): 467–84.

SECTION TWO: INSIDE SCHOOL/FAMILY PARTNERSHIPS

1. Jeannie Oakes, Megan Loef Franke, Karen Hunter Quartz, and John Rogers, "Research for High-Quality Urban Teaching: Defining It, Developing It, Assessing It," *Journal of Teacher Education* 53, no. 3 (2002): 228–34.

2. Norma Gonzalez, Luis C. Moll, and Cathy Amanti, *Funds of Knowledge: Theorizing Practices in Households and Classrooms* (Florence, KY: Lawrence Erlbaum Associates, 2005).

3. C. Pari, "Emergent Discourses: Student Exploration of Cultural Identities," paper presented at the 43rd annual meeting of the Conference on

College Composition and Communication, Cincinnati, OH, March 19–21, 1992.

4. Ronald J. Samuda and Sandra L. Woods, eds., *Perspectives in Immigrant and Minority Education* (Lanham, MD: University Press of America, 1983).

5. Lois Weiner, "Evidence and Inquiry in Teacher Education," *Journal of Teacher Education* 53, no. 3 (2002): 254–61.

SECTION THREE: INSIDE DIFFERENTIATED TEACHING

1. Howard Gardner, *Multiple Intelligences: New Horizons in Theory and Practice* (New York: Basic Books, 2006).

2. John D. Bransford, Ann L. Brown, and Rodney R. Cocking, eds., *How People Learn: Brain, Mind, Experience, and School* (Washington, DC: Commission on Behavioral and Social Sciences and Education, National Research Council, National Academy Press, 2000).

3. Carol Ann Tomlinson, *How to Differentiate Instruction in Mixed-Ability Classrooms*, 2nd ed. (Alexandria, VA: ASCD, 2001).

4. National Committee on Science Education Standards and Assessment, National Research Council, *National Science Education Standards* (Washington, DC: National Academies Press, 1996).

5. Bransford, Brown, and Cocking, *How People Learn*.

6. David Hawkins, "Messing About in Science," in *The Informed Vision: Essays on Learning and Human Nature* (New York: Agathon Press, 1974), 63–75.

7. Thomas S.C. Farrell, *Succeeding with English Language Learners: A Guide for Beginning Teachers* (Thousand Oaks, CA: Corwin Press, 2006); Fred Genesee, Kathryn Lindholm-Leary, William Saunders, and Donna Christian, eds., *Educating English Language Learners: A Synthesis of Research Evidence* (New York: Cambridge University Press, 2007).

8. Tatiana Gordon, *Teaching Young Children a Second Language* (Westport, CT: Praeger, 2007).

9. Ibid., 76.

10. Kathleen Cranley Gallagher and Kelley Mayer, "Enhancing Development and Learning Through Teacher-Child Relationships," *Young Children* 63, no. 6 (2008): 80–87.

11. Judie Haynes, *Getting Started with English Language Learners: How*

Educators Can Meet the Challenge (Alexandria, VA: Association for Supervision and Curriculum Development, 2007).

12. James Cummins, "The Role of Primary Language Development in Promoting Educational Success for Language Minority Students," in *Schooling and Language Minority Students: A Theoretical Framework*, ed. California State Department of Education (Los Angeles: Evaluation, Dissemination and Assessment Center, California State University, 1981).

13. Véronica López Estrada, Leo Gómez, and José Agustín Ruiz-Escalante, "Let's Make Dual Language the Norm," *Educational Leadership* 66, no. 7 (2009): 56.

14. Helen R. Abadiano and Jesse Turner, "Sheltered Instruction: An Empowerment Framework for English Language Learners," *Nera Journal* 38, no. 3 (2002): 50–55; Farrell, *Succeeding with English Language Learners*; Ellen Kottler, Jeffrey A. Kottler, and Chris Street, *English Language Learners in Your Classroom: Strategies That Work* (Thousand Oaks, CA: Corwin Press, 2008); Faridah Pawan, "Content-Area Teachers and Scaffolded Instruction for English Language Learners," *Teaching and Teacher Education* 24, no. 6 (2008): 1450–62; Sharon Adelman Reyes and Trina Lynn Vallone, *Constructivist Strategies for Teaching English Language Learners* (Thousand Oaks, CA: Corwin Press, 2008).

15. Mary A. Avalos, Alina Plasencia, Celina Chavez, and Josefa Rascón, "Modified Guided Reading: Gateway to English as a Second Language and Literacy Learning," *Reading Teacher* 61, no. 4 (2007): 318–29.

16. Linda Chen and Eugenia Mora-Flores, *Balanced Literacy for English Language Learners, K–2* (Portsmouth, NH: Heinemann, 2006); Constance Weaver, *Reading Process and Practice*, 3rd ed. (Portsmouth, NH: Heinemann, 2002).

17. National Association for the Education of Young Children, *Developmentally Appropriate Practice in Early Childhood Programs Serving Children from Birth Through Age 8*, 3rd ed. (Washington, DC: NAEYC, 2009).

SECTION FOUR: INSIDE THE CONSTRAINTS OF URBAN TEACHING

1. Stuart Brown with Christopher Vaughn, *Play: How It Shapes the Brain, Opens the Imagination, and Invigorates the Soul* (New York: Avery, 2010); David Elkind, *The Power of Play: Learning What Comes Naturally* (Cambridge, MA:

Da Capo, 2007); Vivian Gussin Paley, *A Child's Work: The Importance of Fantasy Play* (Chicago: University of Chicago Press, 2005); Jean Tepperman, ed., *Play in the Early Years: Key to School Success* (San Francisco: Bay Area Early Childhood Funders, 2007).

2. National Association for the Education of Young Children, *Developmentally Appropriate Practice in Early Childhood Programs Serving Children from Birth Through Age 8*, 3rd ed. (Washington, DC: NAEYC, 2009).

3. Ibid.

4. J. Amos Hatch and Evelyn B. Freeman, "Who's Pushing Whom? Stress and Kindergarten," *Phi Delta Kappan* 70 (1988): 145–47.

5. Joseph Slate and Ashley Wolff, *Miss Bindergarten Gets Ready for Kindergarten* (London: Puffin Books, 2001).

6. Edward Miller and Joan Almon, *Crisis in the Kindergarten* (College Park, MD: Alliance for Childhood, 2009).

7. lisa spells her name without capital letters.

8. National Association for Sport and Physical Education (NAPSE), "Active Start: A Statement of Physical Activity Guidelines for Children Birth to Five Years," 2nd ed., www.aahperd.org/naspe/standards/nationalguide lines/activestart.cfm.

9. Stephen W. Sanders, *Active for Life: Developmentally Appropriate Movement Programs for Young Children* (Washington, DC: NAEYC, 2002).

10. Craig D. Jerald, *School Culture: The Hidden Curriculum* (Washington DC: Center for Comprehensive School Reform and Improvement, 2006).

11. The names—of the school, teachers, deans, and students—in this chapter are all pseudonyms.

12. Edward W. Chance, Craig Cummins, and Fred Wood, "A Middle School's Approach to Developing an Effective Work Culture," *National Association of Secondary School Principals Bulletin* 80, no. 576 (January 1996): 43–49.

13. Michael Fullan, *Leading in a Culture of Change* (San Francisco: Jossey-Bass, 2001).

14. Terrence E. Deal and Kent D. Peterson, *Shaping School Culture: The School Leader's Role* (San Francisco: Jossey-Bass, 1999), 32.

15. Fullan, *Leading in a Culture of Change*, 97.

CONCLUSION

1. Mihaly Csikszentmihalyi, "The Flow Experience and Its Significance for Human Psychology," in *Optimal Experience: Psychological Studies of Flow in Consciousness* (Cambridge, UK: Cambridge University Press, 1988), 15–35.

2. Beverly Falk, *Developing an Inquiry Stance Toward Teaching* (Stanford, CA: Carnegie Foundation for the Advancement of Teaching, 2007), www .cfkeep.org/html/stitch.php?s=76160188183338&id=8866646912756.

3. Linda Darling-Hammond, *The Flat World and Education* (New York: Teachers College Press, 2010).

4. Marilyn Cochran-Smith and Susan L. Lytle, *Inside/Outside: Teacher Research and Knowledge* (New York: Teachers College Press, 1993); Marilyn Cochran-Smith and Susan L. Lytle, *Inquiry as Stance: Practitioner Research in the Next Generation* (New York: Teachers College Press, 2009); Linda Darling-Hammond and John Bransford, eds., *Preparing Teachers for a Changing World: What Teachers Should Learn and Be Able to Do* (San Francisco: Jossey-Bass, 2005); Michelle Fine, *Charting Urban School Reform: Reflections on Public High Schools in the Midst of Change* (New York: Teachers College Press, 1992); Joseph P. McDonald, *Teaching: Making Sense of an Uncertain Craft* (New York: Teachers College Press, 1992); C. Gordon Wells, *The Meaning Makers: Children Learning Language and Using Language to Learn* (Portsmouth, NH: Heinemann, 1994).

5. Alice McIntyre, "Participatory Action Research and Urban Education: Reshaping the Teacher Preparation Process," *Equity & Excellence in Education* 36, no. 1 (2003): 28–39; Lois Weiner, "Evidence and Inquiry in Teacher Education," *Journal of Teacher Education* 53, no. 3 (2002): 254–61.

6. Jeannie Oakes, Megan Loef Franke, Karen Hunter Quartz, and John Rogers, "Research for High-Quality Urban Teaching: Defining It, Developing It, Assessing It," *Journal of Teacher Education* 53, no. 3 (2002): 231.

7. John Dewey, *Experience and Education* (1938; New York: Macmillan, 1963).

APPENDIX A: HOW THIS BOOK WAS CONSTRUCTED

1. Tracy C. Rock and Barbara B. Levin, "Collaborative Action Research Projects: Enhancing Preservice Teacher Development in Professional Development Schools," *Teacher Education Quarterly* 29, no. 1 (2002): 7.

2. Kelly Chandler-Olcott, "Teacher Researcher as a Self-Extending System for Practitioners," *Teacher Education Quarterly* 29, no. 1 (2002): 23–38.

3. Beverly Falk and Megan Blumenreich, *The Power of Questions: A Guide to Teacher and Student Research* (Portsmouth, NH: Heinemann, 2005).